T0160738

The Reckless Way of Love

The Reckless Way of Love

Notes on Following Jesus

Dorothy Day

Edited by Carolyn Kurtz

PLOUGH PUBLISHING HOUSE

Published by Plough Publishing House
Walden, New York
Robertsbridge, England
Elsmore, Australia
www.plough.com

Plough produces books, a quarterly magazine, and Plough.com to encourage people
and help them put their faith into action. We believe Jesus can transform the world
and that his teachings and example apply to all aspects of life. At the same time, we
seek common ground with all people regardless of their creed.

Plough is the publishing house of the Bruderhof, an international Christian community. The Bruderhof is a fellowship of families and singles practicing radical
discipleship in the spirit of the first church in Jerusalem (Acts 2 and 4). Members
devote their entire lives to serving God, one another, and their neighbors. They
renounce private property and share everything. To learn more about the Bruderhof's
faith, history, and daily life, see Bruderhof.com. (Views expressed by Plough authors
are their own and do not necessarily reflect the position of the Bruderhof.)

Cover art copyright © Julie Lonneman

ISBN 978-0-87486-792-3
22 21 20   5 6 7 8

A catalog record for this book is available from the British Library.

Library of Congress Cataloging-in-Publication Data

Names: Day, Dorothy, 1897-1980, author. | Kurtz, Carolyn, compiler.
Title: The reckless way of love : notes on following Jesus / Dorothy Day ;
   compiled by Carolyn Kurtz.
Description: Walden : Plough Publishing House, 2017. | Includes
   bibliographical references.
Identifiers: LCCN 2016055026 (print) | LCCN 2017002109 (ebook) | ISBN
   9780874867923 (pbk.) | ISBN 9780874867930 (epub) | ISBN 9780874867947
   (mobi) | ISBN 9780874867954 (pdf)
Subjects: LCSH: Christian life--Meditations.
Classification: LCC BV4501.3 .D3947 2017 (print) | LCC BV4501.3 (ebook) | DDC
   248.4/82--dc23
LC record available at https://lccn.loc.gov/2016055026

Printed in the United States of America

Contents

To the Reader   vii

Introduction by D. L. Mayfield   xi

A Way of Faith

1. Help My Unbelief   3

2. To Live by Faith   8

3. Take Heart   13

4. All Will Be Well   18

A Way of Love

5. Love Your Neighbor   25

6. Love the Lord Your God   31

7. Loved by God   37

A Way of Prayer

8. Ask and You Will Receive   43

9. Lord, Teach Me to Pray   49

10. Give Thanks   55

A Way of Life

11. To Walk in His Way   61

12. But How to Love?   68

13. To Love Is to Suffer   81

14. Glory and Beauty   89

A Way of Community

15. Seeing Christ in All Who Come   99

16. Living Together, Working Together   104

17. A Place Where Love Can Grow   112

Notes   121

Bibliography   127

Acknowledgements   128

To the Reader

DOROTHY DAY'S passion for peace and social justice and her dedication to serving the poor are legendary, and her fame continues to grow. Despite her own protests, admirers have petitioned the Vatican to make her a saint. She was one of four people Pope Francis named as truly great Americans. Yet combing through Dorothy's books and articles and her private letters and journals, one discovers an underappreciated dimension of her life. Where did a conflicted young woman find the inner strength to answer the clear call she heard from God? And how did she go on to live such an active, selfless life for so many decades without losing heart or burning out? Unlike other collections, this little volume brings together Dorothy's thoughts on the life of discipleship, the reckless way of love to which Jesus calls his followers. Dorothy's dogged struggle to hold on to faith, her love for those hardest to love, and her rootedness in prayer can guide and encourage each of us in our own attempts to follow more faithfully in the way of Jesus.

The story of Dorothy Day's life has been told well elsewhere, so the briefest biographical sketch here will suffice. There's certainly no better place to start than her own books, *The Long Loneliness* and *Loaves and Fishes*.

Born in Brooklyn in 1897, Dorothy's early years were marked by dramatic twists and turns. There was journalism school, and then a taste of the bohemian Twenties, first in New York City, then Italy, then Hollywood, and finally Staten Island. These were whirlwind years, and left her reeling from a broken marriage, an abortion, and a series of unhappy relationships.

But there was also an unforgettable night in a Greenwich Village bar where her friend, the playwright Eugene O'Neill, recited "The Hound of Heaven" for her – a poem whose obscure but deep message, she later said, eventually brought about her conversion.

In 1926 Dorothy had a baby daughter, Tamar – an event that profoundly changed her. When leftist friends mocked her new interest in the Gospels, Dorothy told them that Jesus promised the new society of justice they were all looking for. If Christians tended to be hypocrites, that was not Jesus' fault. She was determined to give him a try.

In the years that followed, Dorothy did more than try. Shaken by the hopelessness of the unemployed millions during the Depression years, she dropped all ambitions of becoming a famous writer and spent the rest of her life serving the poor (in whose face she saw Jesus), spreading her views of nonviolence (she was imprisoned many times for acts of civil disobedience), and passionately reminding readers through her books and newspaper articles that Christ demanded more than tithes, hats, and flowers on Sunday.

As far as Dorothy could tell, he demanded the readiness to wash vegetables, cut bread, and clean up after hundreds of noisy, often ungrateful guests, day after day, year after year. This she did gladly at the New York Catholic Worker – a communal hospitality house for the unemployed and homeless that she founded with Peter Maurin in 1933.

When Dorothy Day died in 1980 in the cramped Lower East Side room she called home, she owned nothing but a creaking bed, a writing desk, an overflowing bookshelf, a teapot, and a radio. Yet her witness lives on. On a practical level, the work continues today in more than a hundred Catholic Worker houses across the United States and beyond. And as you will find in these pages, we are left with the enduring challenge of her no-nonsense attitude to faith: "The mystery of the poor is this: that they are Jesus, and whatever you do for them you do to him."

Introduction

by D. L. Mayfield

I PICKED UP A BUTTON about a decade ago with a quote attributed to Dorothy Day on it: "If you have two coats, you have stolen one from the poor." I loved this saying, loved the strength of conviction, the easy black-and-white application. I read more about Dorothy and became smitten. Her severe face and warm hands and intense sound bites were so soothing to my soul as I first read of her life and work and the Catholic Worker movement she helped start. I affixed that button to the front of my one orange-plaid corduroy coat and tromped around my neighborhood during the cold, gray Portland winters,

---

D. L. Mayfield, author of Assimilate or Go Home: Notes from a Failed Missionary on Rediscovering Faith, *lives with her husband and children in Portland, Oregon.*

hoping others would read it and be changed. If I am honest, a part of me wanted others to know how radical I was, how I had eschewed the things of the world, how hard I was trying to follow Jesus.

Now, years later, I have three coats: the orange-plaid corduroy still (even though the pockets have ripped), a raincoat (since I live in Oregon), and a longer, warm coat I bought for the three winters I spent in the Midwest. My Dorothy Day button now lives in a junk drawer, because I can't bear to wear it if it isn't true. Should I give one of my coats away? To whom should I give it? I live and work in a refugee and immigrant community; there are dozens of people I know who could use a coat. How do I pick? How do I navigate the enormity of the needs of the world, and my own response to them? I still don't know. And yet, even as I think these thoughts and feel like a failed radical, the words and life of Dorothy Day mean more to me than ever.

I take some comfort in knowing that Dorothy struggled with these same questions and contradictions throughout her life. Her feelings, I suspect, were complicated, since she was a unique and complex woman. She was driven, proud, dogmatic. She lived with fierce conviction in solidarity with the poor. She was also unsure, doubtful, and depressed from time to time due to the enormity of the suffering surrounding her. From a young age, Dorothy showed evidence of both her passion for justice and her quick mind. She was an activist, a sharp student, a curator of deep conversations. Her biographer, Robert Coles, noted that she was quick to dismiss her early life, preferring to talk instead of her conversion to Catholicism and how she met Peter Maurin, with whom she cofounded the Catholic Worker's newspaper and houses of hospitality. But the threads of her personality and strong convictions and engaging writing style were already all there, and her years of struggle and wandering no doubt contributed to her profound empathy for those who suffer.

Even in this collection of her writings you can find diverging thoughts – she writes of always hiding her sadness, and also of the importance of feeling the full force of emotions. These contradictions reassure me, reminding me that she is human like me, and invite me into her journey. Instead of holding her up as a saint to admire, these writings instead portray an ordinary person simply trying to walk the road of following Christ. In documenting this continual journey, Dorothy Day ended up talking constantly about struggle and cultural isolation. As she writes in her autobiography, *The Long Loneliness,* "We have all known the long loneliness and we have learned that the only solution is love and that love comes with community."

Community is a buzzword these days, primarily for people who don't quite understand how taxing true interdependence can be. As someone impatient with platitudes, I have always been drawn to Dorothy Day's kind of community. I was electrified by the way she wrote about the poor and the suffering and the proper response of the Christian (self-sacrificial love). And I was challenged by the example set by her houses of hospitality, where the homeless and desperate could stay and people could live and work side by side.

Robert Coles remembers how, the first time he met Dorothy, she was chatting with an intoxicated older woman. She looked up and saw Coles waiting and asked him, "Were you waiting to talk to one of us?" Already quite famous, she didn't assume Coles wanted to talk to her more than he might want to talk to her neighbor. With that simple question, Coles says, "she cut through layers of self-importance, a lifetime of bourgeois privilege, and scraped the hard bone of pride" (*Dorothy Day: A Radical Devotion,* xviii). Dorothy Day had absorbed the beliefs of her beloved Christ so deeply that she truly lived as if everyone was of equal importance in a world that applauds hierarchy and prestige.

I am not Catholic, and yet Dorothy Day's attitude to faith has impacted me greatly. I grew up in a conservative church that emphasized personal piety and correct doctrine, but at some point those no longer seemed sufficient as guidelines for life lived in community. Living and working with refugees, the challenges that the poor face soon overwhelmed me – they were the splash of cold water that woke me from my stupor. It was then that I discovered Dorothy Day's books, and she became a guide into a wild new world of following Christ on a downwardly mobile path.

And oh, would I need some wisdom and guidance for that journey! For years I had been too busy "working for the Lord" to spend much time learning from others, especially others who were different from me. I'm a doer. I like to get my hands and feet in the mess of the world. This, I'll admit, is why the writings of Dorothy Day reached out and grabbed me initially. I identified with her iron will and the practical ways she strove to meet the real and tangible needs of those affected by poverty and war.

What made her such a radical? Was it the kerchief she wore in her hair? Her intense writing style? Her involvement in politics while refusing to be conscripted into any political party? Was it her lack of material possessions or her firm belief in the inherent dignity of all people? Or her commitment to the church despite her differences and disappointments? I thought it was a combination of all of these things when I first discovered Dorothy in my early twenties. Now, over a decade later, I have a different answer: her radicalness stems from the transformative love of Christ she experienced throughout her very long and sometimes very lonely life.

Wherever she turned, Dorothy saw Christ up on his cross. One of her rules of life was to seek the face of Christ in the poor. She found him there, and in so many other places. Christ was the person in line for soup and bread; Christ was the drunk woman having the same conversation over and over again; Christ was the enemy combatant; Christ was the priest she disagreed with; Christ was the young person begging for spiritual direction; Christ was in every reader she wrote for, including me, including you.

Dorothy Day's eyes were first opened to the inequalities of our world when she saw the long lines of people waiting for bread during the Great Depression. Mine were opened the day I realized my refugee neighbors had only been given eight months of assistance by the government and were now expected to be assimilated as fully-functioning members of society. For non-literate, tribal, rural, Muslim Africans plopped down in the middle of Portland, this was ludicrous at best and heart-breaking in reality. I was nineteen years old and dove headfirst into helping these refugee families navigate life in America. I moved into their community and tried to hitch my life to theirs. I ran homework clubs and art classes and English classes. I asked churches and friends and family members to get involved. But life moved on. Volunteers stopped showing up. People weren't as grateful as I had hoped they would be. Countless hours in waiting rooms and, on hold, trying to navigate bureaucracies did not feel exactly radical. I tried to help everyone as best as I could, but I was failing miserably.

"She is one of our many failures," writes Dorothy Day in a letter to a friend, referencing a woman who left the house of hospitality, most likely to more drink and chaos. Life in community with broken people will always include such disappointments. But they can be met with resilience, and with a faith in the eternal significance of a life lived with the suffering. Such a life will never be easy or tidy; the work is endless and will always stretch on before us.

So how do we go forward? If I am honest, at first I was a bit impatient with this short book of Dorothy Day's writings. "Where is the work?" I thought. "Where are all the inspiring stories of her interactions with the poor, the causes of equality that she championed, her countercultural lifestyle choices?" I was, and remain, hungry to hear stories of God's kingdom coming at the margins of society; I want first-person accounts of the glories and heartbreaks at the frontlines. But here in this volume we find someone who at first blush does not seem all that radical. Instead, Dorothy Day is a woman who reads the Scripture constantly, prays, goes to church, partakes in the sacraments, bakes bread and mops floors, writes letters to her friends. She seems very pious, very devout. She comes across as a borderline mystic, sometimes even a bit ethereal, someone who uses religious imagery constantly.

But we know how entrenched her life was in the lives of the very people Jesus said would be blessed – the poor, the sick, the sad, the oppressed – and her spiritual reflections reflect that reality. They spring up from a place of love, not distance. Dorothy Day was not just a radical at the frontlines, writing screeds and organizing protests (although she did all that too). She was a woman bound to daily service in community, deeply committed to rhythms of prayer, reflection, and solitude. She was someone who wanted to live for Christ her entire life, and so she dedicated hers to growing in awareness and understanding of the love of Jesus.

It still astonishes me that it can be this simple and yet so hard to obey. The love of Christ is everything. Not the work, not the needs, not the good intentions. It is entering into the wound of love of Christ on the cross, and being transformed by it. Dorothy writes: "How can we ever give up thinking and longing for love, talking of it, preparing ourselves for it, reading of it, studying about it? It is really a great faith in love that never dies." Her "work" was her relationship with Christ.

This should cause us to question ourselves. Why am I exhausted by mothering small children while trying to create places of welcome in my neighborhood? Why have so many of my friends who have worked hard to bring justice into the world also faltered, their light dimmed after a few short years? How many other would-be disciples could say the same? What is it we truly want for this one life we are given? A frustrated life of service where we drag ourselves along by the bootstraps? Or a sustainable life that is constantly renewed by the inexhaustible love of Christ and our connection to him?

In these pages, Dorothy Day invites us into the latter. She calls on us to lay down our burdens and instead link arms with other Christ-followers throughout the centuries. The famous images show her fierce and strong and often alone, but in reality she was connected to a great number of saints – through her books and her prayers and her interactions with her neighbors. Here she found the strength to move forward until the very last moment. She did not view herself as an individual, or a radical, or a prophet; she was one of a great many people whom Christ loved. And like a gorgeous, broken vessel, she was filled with that love day after day and spilled it out wherever she went.

Even now the cares of the world weigh on me. The suffering of people is real and devastating, especially for immigrants, refugees, people of color, and those who are not valued as productive citizens. I am surrounded by these people, and here I sit with three coats hanging up in my closet, wondering at what I am to do.

And yet even now, I know. I will pray for faith, and for love, and for peace. I will fight to carve out space in my life for Christ above all else, to be in community with him and the ones he loves. I still long to be like Dorothy Day, but not in the ways I used to. I don't want to be radical anymore; instead I long to be sustainable, to remain steadfast. I want to walk faithfully in the direction of my Lord, and I don't want to stop until my very last breath. As Dorothy writes, "Our arms are linked – we try to be neighbors of his, and to speak up for his principles. That's a lifetime's job."

A Way of Faith

If you have faith as small as a mustard seed, you can say to this mountain, "Move from here to there" and it will move. Nothing will be impossible for you.

MATTHEW 17:20-21

I

Help My Unbelief

Now faith is confidence in what we hope for and assurance about what we do not see.

HEBREWS 11:1

I REMEMBER the first radio I had in the early twenties, constructed for me by Willy Green, a twelve-year-old, out of a cigar box, a crystal, a bit of wire, an aerial, and earphones. Manipulated properly, from my seashore bungalow in Staten Island, I could hear a presidential campaign, Saturday p.m. broadcasts, football, and, miracle of miracles, symphonic music. That little radio was a miracle box. I could not understand it. If *this* is possible, anything is. . . .

So I could take on faith the truths of Christianity, the church, the sacraments. My heart swelled with gratitude.

Faith came to me just like that, and the need to adore.

I could not understand the mechanism of the little box with its crystal, set like a jewel to be touched by a bit of wire. It was a miracle to hear voices of people in conversation, a symphony orchestra playing Beethoven.

If I could not understand scientific truths, why should I worry about understanding spiritual truths of religion? I wanted to say yes, this is true.

THE CEREMONY OF BAPTISM is certainly impressive, with the priest beginning, "What dost thou ask of the church of God?" and the sponsor answering for the child, "Faith."

It made me think of my days of struggle coming into the church, how I did not know whether or not I had faith or believed, or just wanted to believe. Things that I questioned I just put out of my mind then, and reconciled myself with the thought, "After all, why should I expect to understand everything? That would be heaven indeed." I knew that if I waited to understand, if I waited to get rid of all my doubts, I would never be ready. So I went in all haste one December day right after Christmas and was baptized a Catholic. I did not think of it at the time – I understood so little that when I went to be baptized I asked for faith. But I knew that prayer, "Lord, I believe, help thou mine unbelief" (Mark 9:24), and that comforted me.

I BELIEVED in Jesus Christ – that he is *real,* that he is the son of God, that he came here, that he entered history, and that he is still here, with us, all the time, through his church, through the sacraments of the church.

FAITH CAME before understanding. And faith is a gift of God. It cannot be imparted by any other person. I cannot give it to you. Only God.

YOU ARE CERTAINLY going through the sorrowful mysteries. But if you don't go through them to the glorious, you will be a hollow man, and considered an opportunist and a fraud. I am putting it as strong as I am able, and hate doing it, but to me the faith is the strongest thing in my life and I can never be grateful enough for the joy I have had for the gift of faith, my Catholicism.

LIFE WOULD BE UTTERLY UNBEARABLE if we thought we were going nowhere, that we had nothing to look forward to. The greatest gift life can offer would be a faith in God and a hereafter. Why don't we have it? Perhaps like all gifts it must be struggled for. "God, I believe" (or rather, "I must believe or despair"). "Help thou my unbelief." "Take away my heart of stone and give me a heart of flesh."

I wrote the above lines when I felt the urgent need for faith, but there were too many people passing through my life – too many activities – too much pleasure (not happiness).

FAITH, MORE PRECIOUS THAN GOLD, is a gift. We cannot give it to each other, but certainly we can pray God to give it to others. Péguy* wrote: "When we get to heaven, God is going to say to us, 'Where are the others?'"

We must not judge the church by the man, by the human element. I must pray for priests, pray for conversions, and I must not seem in my writing to be telling others what to do – but I must be speaking of myself, for

* Charles Pierre Péguy, 1873–1914, French poet and writer

my own peace of soul. Not trying for conversions to the church, not proselytizing, but leaving things to God, who wills that all men be saved, and can give his divine life through any channel.

IT IS THE FIRST LETTER OF PETER, chapter 1, which engrosses me, about belief in Jesus – in the power of his holy name. And my own joy and gratitude to him, and the whole problem of faith, which is so precious it must be tried as though by fire. I pray daily for my grandchildren, for my children, that God will draw them to himself, through Jesus, as he has promised. And you know I pray for you.

2

To Live by Faith

Have faith in God. . . . Truly I tell you, if anyone says to this mountain, "Go, throw yourself into the sea," and does not doubt in their heart but believes that what they say will happen, it will be done for them.

MARK 11:22-23

FAITH IS REQUIRED when we speak of obedience. Faith in a God who created us, a God who is Father, Son, and Holy Spirit. Faith in a God to whom we owe obedience for the very reason that we have been endowed with freedom to obey or disobey. Love, beauty, truth, all the attributes of God which we see reflected about us in creatures, in the very works of man himself, whether it is bridges or symphonies wrought by his hands, fill our hearts with such wonder and gratitude that we cannot help but obey and worship.

Lord, I believe, help thou my unbelief. My faith may be the size of a mustard seed, but even so, even aside from its potential, it brings with it a beginning of love, an inkling of love, so intense that human love with all its heights and depths pales in comparison.

Even seeing through a glass darkly makes one want to obey, to do all the Beloved wishes, to follow him to Siberia, to Antarctic wastes, to the desert, to prison, to give up one's life for one's brothers since he said, "Inasmuch as ye have done it unto one of the least of these my brethren, ye have done it unto me."

"WITHOUT FAITH it is impossible to please God" (Heb. 11:6). Faith that works through love is the mark of the supernatural life. God always gives us a chance to show our preference for him. With Abraham it was to sacrifice his only son. With me it was to give up my married life with Forster. You do these things blindly, not because it is your natural inclination – you are going against nature when you do them – but because you wish to live in conformity with the will of God.

THESE HOT AUGUST DAYS when we are so tired
I wake up wondering what we will do in the dead of
winter – it seems to get harder in anticipation and yet I
know by experience how one should take the hardships
as they come, day by day, one by one, rather than look
forward, or backward either. To live in the *now* is to be
like little children. To be utterly dependent on our Father
is to be like little children.

WE MAY BE LIVING on the verge of eternity – but
that should not make us dismal. The early Christians
rejoiced to think that the end of the world was near, as
they thought. Over and over again, even to the Seventh
Day Adventists of our time, people have been expecting
the end of the world. Are we so unready to face God? Are
we so avid for joys here that we perceive so darkly those
to come?

It is hard to think of these things. It is not to be understood; we cannot expect to understand. We must just live
by faith, and the faith that God is good, that all times are
in his hands, must be tried as though by fire.

THE FIRST JOB of the Christian, it seems to me, is to
grow in faith in God – in his power, in the conviction

that we are all held in the hollow of his hand. He is our safeguard and defense. This faith we must pray for does away with fear, which paralyzes all effort – fear of losing a job, of hunger, of eviction, as well as fear of bodily violence and the blows of insult and contempt. Let us respect each other as well as love each other.

I do not want to play down martyrdoms, but to keep in mind always, "Father, forgive them for they know not what they do." God loves all men. "God wills that all men be saved." But we have that great and glorious gift of free will, which distinguishes man from the beast, the power of choice, and man often chooses evil because it has the semblance of the good, because it seems to promise happiness.

TO GROW IN FAITH in God, in Christ, in the Holy Spirit, that is the thing. Without him we can do nothing. With him we can do all things.

He will raise up leaders who will know how to combat the secular, or rather how to integrate the spiritual and material, so that life will be a more balanced one of joy and sorrow.

I HAVE HAD SO MANY YEARS of experience of how God takes care of those who trust him. He is unfailing and will send us what we need. . . . Sometimes we are driven by circumstances to do what God wants rather than what we want and afterwards know that it is all to the good.

3

Take Heart

Wait for the Lord; be strong and take heart and wait for the Lord.

PSALM 27:14

WITHOUT THE SACRAMENTS of the church, primarily the Eucharist, the Lord's Supper as it is sometimes called, I certainly do not think that I could go on. I do not always approach it from need, or with joy and thanksgiving. After thirty-eight years of almost daily communion, one can confess to a routine, but it is like a routine of taking daily food. But Jesus himself told us at that last supper, "Do this in memory of me"

(Luke 22:19). He didn't say daily, of course. But he said, "as often as you drink this wine and eat this bread," we would be doing it in memory of him (1 Cor. 11:25). And this morning I rejoiced to see those words in the Gospel of Saint Luke. He said, "How I have longed to eat this Passover with you before my death!" The old Douay version has it, "With desire I have desired to eat this pasch with you, before I suffer" (Luke 22:15).

Desire, to me, always meant an intense craving, a longing, a yearning which was a joy in itself to experience.

DO WHAT COMES TO HAND. Whatsoever thy hand finds to do, do it with all thy might. After all, God is with us. It shows too much conceit to trust to ourselves, to be discouraged at what we ourselves can accomplish. It is lacking in faith in God to be discouraged. After all, we are going to proceed with his help. We offer him what we are going to do. If he wishes it to prosper, it will. We must depend solely on him. Work as though everything depended on ourselves, and pray as though everything depended on God, as Saint Ignatius says. . . .

I suppose it is a grace not to be able to have time to take or derive satisfaction in the work we are doing. In what time I have, my impulse is to self-criticism and examination of conscience, and I am constantly humiliated at my own imperfections and at my halting progress. Perhaps I deceive myself here, too, and excuse my lack of recollection. But I do know how small I am and how little I can do and I beg You, Lord, to help me, for I cannot help myself.

IN A WAY your letter was very disquieting – you seemed so overcome by failure and defeat. You seem much under the influence of Péguy. I have been quoting that for years – "'Where are the others?' God will say" – and I do believe that we have to work for others. But we are sowing the seed and it is up to him to bring the increase. It is all in his hands, and we must keep ourselves in peace, first of all. That is where peace begins. He is our peace.

THIS MORNING the only gleam of consolation I had was that when God sends all these troubles and sufferings to the families, he is sending just what they need, to prune them down, so that they bear fruit. If I didn't believe that, I'd be unhappy indeed. How he must love you to be so intent on sending what you need, spiritually. If all were going well and smoothly, it would be really dangerous.

TODAY THE ATMOSPHERE is very heavy. Rain threatens. So often one is overcome with a tragic sense of the meaninglessness of our lives – patience, patience, and the very word means suffering. Endurance, perseverance, sacrament of the present moment, the sacrament of duty. One must keep on reassuring oneself of these things. And repeat acts of faith. "Lord, I believe, help thou my unbelief." We are placed here; why? To know him and so love him, serve him by serving others, and so attain to eternal life and joy, understanding, etc.

WE KNOW how powerless we are, all of us, against the power of wealth and government and industry and science. The powers of this world are overwhelming. Yet it is hoping against hope and believing, in spite of "unbelief," crying by prayer and by sacrifice, daily, small, constant sacrificing of one's own comfort and cravings – these are the things that count.

And old as I am, I see how little I have done, how little I have accomplished along these lines.

ONE TIME I was traveling and far from home and lonely, and I awoke in the night almost on the verge of weeping with a sense of futility, of being unloved and unwanted. And suddenly the thought came to me of my importance as a daughter of God, daughter of a king, and I felt a sureness of God's love and at the same time a conviction that one of the greatest injustices, if one can put it that way, which one can do to God is to distrust his love, not realize his love. God so loved me that he gave his only begotten son. "If a mother will forget her children, never will I forget thee." Such tenderness. And with such complete ingratitude we forget the Father and his love!

4

All Will Be Well

*We boast in the hope of the glory of God. Not only so, but
we also glory in our sufferings, because we know that
suffering produces perseverance; perseverance, character;
and character, hope.*

ROMANS 5:2−4

THE GRACE OF HOPE, this consciousness that there
is in every person *that which is of God,* comes and goes
in a rhythm like that of the sea. The Spirit blows where it
listeth, and we travel through deserts and much darkness
and doubt. We can only make that act of faith, "Lord, I
believe, because I want to believe." We must remember

that faith, like love, is an act of the will, an act of preference. God speaks, he answers these cries in the darkness
as he always did. He is incarnate today in the poor, in the
bread we break together. We know him and each other in
the breaking of bread.

I HAVE FALLEN IN LOVE many a time in the fall
of the year. I mean those times when body and soul
are revived and, in the keen clear air of autumn after a
hot exhausting summer, I feel new strength to see, to
"know" clearly, and to love, to look upon my neighbor
and to love. Almost to be taken out of myself. I do not
mean being in love with a particular person. I mean
that quality of in-loveness that may brush like a sweet
fragrance, a sound faintly heard, a sense of the beauty of
one particular human being, or even one aspect of life. It
may be an intuition of immortality, of the glory of God,
of his presence in the world. But it is almost impossible to
put into words. The point is that it is general rather than
particular, though it may come as a reminder, this flash
of understanding, of recognition, with the reading of a
particular book, or hearing some strain of music.

It is tied up in some way also with the sense of
hope, and an understanding of hope. How can we live

without it, as a supernatural virtue, "hoping against hope," during this dark period of violence and suffering throughout the world?

I am bold in trying to express the inexpressible, to write of happiness, even of joy that comes, regardless of age, color, or condition of servitude, to us all. Regardless of failures, regardless even of the sufferings of others. If we did not have this hope, this joy, this love, how could we help others? How could we have the strength to hold on to them, to hold them up when they are drowning in sorrow, suffocating in blackness, almost letting go of life, life which we know with a sure knowledge is precious, which is something to hold to, be grateful for, to reverence.

HOPE AND FAITH – how they are tied up together. And love – which desires the best for others. Not an emotional love, a self-gratifying love, but a love which surpasses dislike – that dislike occasioned by dishonesty, and offenses like drug pushing and sex irregularities, in other words, corruption, impurity. Dislike is a mild word – hatred would be better. How to hate the sin and love the sinner! Our God is a consuming fire in what he expects of us – the impossible. Yet he has promised,

"I can do all things in Him who strengthens me" (Phil. 4:13). Not achieving holy indifference, but to bear in peace the suffering, to overcome fears as to the outcome of all this, to know that he can bring good out of evil, that "all will be well" (Julian of Norwich).*

LIFE GETS HARDER. How hard it is to down the violence in our own natures – to "be present" and suffer and have faith and hope. To keep an appearance at least of calm confidence that "all will be well, all will be very well." Must read Julian of Norwich again.

* Julian of Norwich, 1342–1416, English anchoress, mystic, and theologian

A Way of Love

A new command I give you: Love one another. As I have loved you, so you must love one another.

5

Love Your Neighbor

"Love your neighbor as yourself." Love does no harm to a neighbor. Therefore love is the fulfillment of the law.

ROMANS 13:9–10

THERE IS A CHARACTER in *The Plague* by Albert Camus who says that he is tired of hearing about men dying for an idea. He would like to hear about a man dying for love for a change. He goes on to say that men have forgotten how to love, that all they seem to be thinking of these days is learning how to kill. Man, he says, seems to have lost the capacity for love.

What is God but love? What is religion without love? We read of the saints dying for love, and we wonder what they mean. There was a silly verse I used to hear long ago: "Men have died from time to time, and worms have eaten them, but not for love." It comes from *As You Like It.* And nowadays in this time of war and preparing for war, we would agree, except for the saints. Yes, they have died for love of God. But Camus's character would say, "I mean for love of man." Our Lord did that, but most people no longer believe in him. It is hard to talk to people about God if they do not believe in him. So one can talk and write of love. People want to believe in that even when they are all but convinced that it is an illusion. (It would be better still to love rather than to write about it. It would be more convincing.)

LOVE AND EVER MORE LOVE is the only solution to every problem that comes up. If we love each other enough, we will bear with each other's faults and burdens. If we love enough, we are going to light that fire in the hearts of others. And it is love that will burn out the sins and hatreds that sadden us. It is love that will make us want to do great things for each other. No sacrifice and no suffering will then seem too much.

Yes, I see only too clearly how bad people are. I wish I did not see it so. It is my own sins that give me such clarity. If I did not bear the scars of so many sins to dim my sight and dull my capacity for love and joy, then I would see Christ more clearly in you all.

I cannot worry much about your sins and miseries when I have so many of my own. I can only love you all, poor fellow travelers, fellow sufferers. I do not want to add one least straw to the burden you already carry. My prayer from day to day is that God will so enlarge my heart that I will see you all, and live with you all, in his love.

IN CHRIST'S HUMAN LIFE, there were always a few who made up for the neglect of the crowd. The shepherds did it; their hurrying to the crib atoned for the people who would flee from Christ. The wise men did it; their journey across the world made up for those who refused to stir one hand's breadth from the routine of their lives to go to Christ. Even the gifts the wise men brought have in themselves an obscure recompense and atonement for what would follow later in this child's life. For they brought gold, the king's emblem, to make up for the crown of thorns that he would wear; they offered incense, the symbol of praise, to make up for the mockery and the spitting; they gave him myrrh, to heal and soothe, and he was wounded from head to foot and no one bathed his wounds. The women at the foot of the cross did it too, making up for the crowd who stood by and sneered.

We can do it too, exactly as they did. We are not born too late. We do it by seeing Christ and serving Christ in friends and strangers, in everyone we come in contact with.

JESUS CHRIST knew what was in man. I was not baptized until I was twelve, but I had a conscience. I knew what was in man too. But I had too a tremendous faith in man as a temple of the holy Ghost, in man made [in] the image and likeness of God, a little less than the angels. Truly I did not want to know good and evil. I wanted to know, to believe only the good. I wanted to believe that man could right wrongs, could tilt the lance, could love and espouse the cause of his brother because "an injury to one was an injury to all." I never liked the appeal to enlightened self-interest. I wanted to love my fellows; I loved the poor with compassion. I could not be happy unless I shared poverty, lived as they did, suffered as they did.

"MY SOUL hath thirsted after the strong living God; when shall I come and appear before the face of God?" (Psalm 42:2). But the Psalmist also says, "In death there is no one that is mindful of thee." So it made me happy that I could be with my mother the last few weeks of her life, and for the last ten days at her bedside daily and hourly. Sometimes I thought to myself that it was like being present at a birth to sit by a dying person and see their intentness on what is happening to them. It almost seems that one is absorbed in a struggle, a fearful, grim, physical struggle, to breathe, to swallow, to live. And so, I kept thinking to myself, how necessary it is for one of their loved ones to be beside them, to pray for them, to offer up prayers for them unceasingly, as well as to do all those little offices one can. When my daughter was a little tiny girl, she said to me once, "When I get to be a great big woman and you are a little tiny girl, I'll take care of you," and I thought of that when I had to feed my mother by the spoonful and urge her to eat her custard. How good God was to me, to let me be there. I had prayed so constantly that I would be beside her when she died; for years I had offered up that prayer. And God granted it quite literally. I was there, holding her hand, and she just turned her head and sighed. That was her last breath, that little sigh, and her hand was warm in mine for a long time after.

It was hard to talk about dying, but every now and then we did. But I told her that we could no more imagine the life beyond the grave than a blind man could imagine colors. We talked about faith, and how we could go just so far in our reasoned belief, and that our knowledge was like a bridge which came to an end, so that it did not reach the other shore. A wonderful prayer, that one. "I believe, O God. Help thou mine unbelief."

6

Love the Lord Your God

Love the Lord your God with all your heart and with all your soul and with all your strength.

HOW MUCH did I hear of religion as a child? Very little, and yet my heart leaped when I heard the name of God. I do believe every soul has a tendency toward God. "As soon as man recalls the Godhead, a certain sweet movement fills his heart. . . . Our understanding has never such great joy as when thinking of God," Saint Francis de Sales* writes.

* Francis de Sales, 1567–1622, Catholic bishop and spiritual director

BUT ALWAYS the glimpses of God came most when I was alone. Objectors cannot say that it was fear of loneliness and solitude and pain that made me turn to him. It was in those few years when I was alone and most happy that I found him. I found him at last through joy and thanksgiving, not through sorrow.

The next five selections are Dorothy's personal notes from a retreat she attended during summer of 1948.

OUR PRAYER SHOULD BE, "Speak Lord, for thy servant heareth." We should ask God to teach us the secrets of his love. Insist on this love with importunity. No other love is happy unless it finds its roots in this. Loving God seems to be loving nothing? But there is a definite way. We must learn the rules. There is infinite happiness waiting. Also, it will free us from the slavery of other loves. God is nothing else but love. "Where love is, there God is." All other loves pale in comparison. Our nature is not built for so strong a love, so we must change our nature. "Enlarge thou my heart, that thou mayest enter in." How can you tell if a person loves you? By their thoughts, words, and deeds. Our love is made up of our actions. There is a conformity, a union of desires, tastes, deeds. Many people want to and do make sacrifices, but there is not much change in the temperature of their love for God. . . . We are children of God. Grace is participation in the life of God. Human life is natural to us. Supernatural life is added unto us. We have new powers.

OUR GREATEST DANGER is not our sins but our indifference. We must be in love with God. It is not so much to change what we are doing, but our intention, our motive. It is not sufficient that we refrain from insulting a person; we must love. . . . When we say that we love God with our whole heart, it means whole. We must love only God. And that sets up the triangle – God, the soul, the world.

The wife wants the husband's whole love. Suppose a husband pays no attention to his wife, and we say, "Well, he does not beat you, does he? You should be satisfied that he does not kill you. What are you complaining about?"

It is the same with God. He is not just content that we are not in a state of mortal sin. . . . We must do more than just stay in a state of grace.

ALL OTHER LOVES I have must be a sample of the love of God. All the world and everything in it must be samples of the love of God. We must love the world intensely, but not for itself. We are human beings; we do not cease to be human beings, but we are baptized human beings. At death we are going to join God with the amount of love we have gathered for him. What we have when we die we will have for all eternity.

TWO PEOPLE who are deeply in love are thinking of each other all the time and what they can do for each other. So we must be with God. The love of God is more intense than any human love. Keep asking for this love.

RESULTS? Are we to be as perfect as Saint Francis, as Saint John, as Saint Peter? No, we are expected to be perfect "as our heavenly Father is perfect." Because God wants it. We must aim high because he says so. Lay up for yourselves treasures in heaven. What do you think about all day? Worldly things? There is your heart. Are you concerned about health, bodily goods? There your heart is. If one falls in love, all the habits of life are ruled by that love – letters, telephone calls, whatever we do.

Suppose, on getting married, a woman says, "Are you sure you can supply me with clothes, with food?" We are in love with God; we will have what we need. "Behold the birds of the air: they neither sow, nor reap, nor gather into barns" (Matt. 6:26).

God is a sensitive lover. God will not force you to choose him. It is an insult to God to worry so about the things of the world.

WHEN WE ARE ASKED to show our love for God, our desire for him, when he asks us as Jesus asked Peter, "Lovest thou me?" we have to give proof of it. "Lovest thou me more than these, more than any human companionship, more than any human love?" It is not filth and ugliness, drugs and drink and perversion he is asking us to prefer him to. He is asking us to prefer him to all beauty and loveliness. To all other love. He is giving us a chance to prove our faith, our hope, our charity. It is as hard and painful as Abraham's ordeal, when he thought he was asked to perform a human sacrifice and immolate his son.

"EYE HATH NOT SEEN, nor ear heard what God hath prepared for those who love him" (1 Cor. 2:9). But do I love him? The only test is, am I willing to sacrifice present happiness and present love for him? I have done it once, and thereby kept them. The thing is, one must keep doing it, day after day, beginning over and over, to count all things but dross compared to the life of the spirit which alone is able to bring joy, overcome fear – "Love casts out fear" (1 John 4:18). "I know that my redeemer liveth, and in my flesh I shall see God my Savior" (Job 19:25–26). "I believe, help thou my unbelief." Most of the time I am as sure of these things as I am of my own life. And as for those periods of desert and doubt, there is so much in the line of inescapable duty that one can work one's way through them.

I AM CONVINCED that prayer and austerity, prayer and self-sacrifice, prayer and fasting, prayer and vigils, and prayer and marches are the indispensable means. . . . And love.

All these means are useless unless animated by love.

"Love your enemies." That is the hardest saying of all.

Please, Father in heaven who made me, take away my heart of stone and give me a heart of flesh to love my enemy.

It is a terrible thought – "we love God as much as the one we love the least."

7

Loved by God

This is love: not that we loved God, but that he loved us
and sent his Son as an atoning sacrifice for our sins.

1 JOHN 4:10

I AM TERRIBLY AFRAID of intruding on people's
personal inner lives. But when I write personally about
myself and my own religious feelings, it is because my
heart yearns toward others, that they may know the happiness I do.

Well, my great comfort is that God loves them more
than I do, and God, our Father, wills that all men be
saved, and when I pray, "Thy will be done," I'm praying
for their salvation.

THERE ARE ALL KINDS OF FEAR, and I certainly pray to be delivered from the fear of my brother; I pray to grow in the love that casts out fear. To grow in love of God and man, and to live by this charity, that is the problem. We must love our enemy, not because we fear war but because God loves him.

DO YOU REMEMBER that little story that Grushenka tells in *The Brothers Karamazov?*

Once upon a time there was a peasant woman, and a very wicked woman she was. And she died and did not leave a single good deed behind. The devils caught her and plunged her into the lake of fire. So her guardian angel stood and wondered what good deed of hers he could remember to tell God. "She once pulled up an onion in her garden," said he, "and gave it to a beggar woman." And God answered: "You take that onion then, hold it out to her in the lake, and let her take hold and be pulled out. And if you pull her out of the lake, let her come to Paradise, but if the onion breaks, then the woman must stay where she is." The angel ran to the woman and held out the onion to her. "Come," said he, "catch hold, and I'll pull you out." And he began cautiously pulling her out. He had just pulled her right out when the other sinners in the lake, seeing how she was being drawn out, began catching hold of her so as to be pulled out with her. But she was a very wicked woman and she began kicking them. "I'm to be pulled out, not you. It's my onion, not yours." As soon as she said that, the onion broke. And the woman fell into the lake and she is burning there to this day. So the angel wept and went away.

Sometimes in thinking and wondering at God's goodness to me, I have thought that it was because I gave away an onion. Because I sincerely loved his poor, he taught me to know him. And when I think of the little I ever did, I am filled with hope and love for all those others devoted to the cause of social justice.

WOKE UP this a.m. with the feeling very strong – I belong to Someone to whom I owe devotion. Recalled early love and the joyous sense of being not my own, but of belonging to someone who loved me completely.

WHAT IS GOD BUT LOVE? . . . It is hard to believe in this love because it is a tremendous love. "It is a terrible thing to fall into the hands of the living God"

(Heb. 10:31). If we do once catch a glimpse of it, we are afraid of it. Once we recognize that we are sons of God, that the seed of divine life has been planted in us at baptism, we are overcome by that obligation placed upon us of growing in the love of God.

THE LOVE OF GOD and man becomes the love of equals, as the love of the bride and bridegroom is the love of equals, and not the love of the sheep for the shepherd, or the servant for the master, or the son for the father. We may stand at times in the relationship of servant, and at other times in that of son, as far as our feelings go and in our present state. But the relationship we hope to attain to is that of the love of the Canticle of Canticles. If we cannot deny the *self* in us, kill the self-love, as He has commanded, and put on the Christ life, then God will do it for us. We must become like him. Love must go through these purgations.

LOVE MUST BE TRIED and tested and proved. It must be tried as though by fire, and fire burns. "It is a dreadful thing to fall into the hands of the living God."

A Way of Prayer

*When you pray, go into your room, close the door and pray
to your Father, who is unseen.*

MATTHEW 6:6

8

Ask and You Will Receive

Until now you have not asked for anything in my name.
Ask and you will receive, and your joy will be complete.

JOHN 16:24

DOES GOD HAVE a set way of prayer, a way that he
expects each of us to follow? I doubt it. I believe some
people – lots of people – pray through the witness of their
lives, through the work they do, the friendships they
have, the love they offer people and receive from people.
Since when are *words* the only acceptable form of prayer?

BEING ON ONE'S KNEES is not entirely necessary.
That was an attitude of reverence from courtly days. Jews

stood. When our Lord went into the desert or up on the mountain to pray, he was not necessarily always on his knees. One can walk with the Lord. I remember how I used to pray, walking on the beach. . . . I do not have to retire to my room to pray. It is enough to get out and walk in the wilderness of the streets.

I DO BELIEVE IN A PERSONAL GOD, because I too have had revelations, answers to my questions, to my prayers, and if the answer fails to come, which is usually the case because God wants us to work out our own salvation, I have that assurance God gave Saint Paul and he passed on to us, "My grace is sufficient for you."

And what is grace? Participation in the divine life. And that participation means for me light and understanding and conviction, of course only occasionally, but strong enough to carry me along, to lift me up out of depression, discouragement, uncertainty, doubt.

IF WE HAVE FAILED to achieve Peter's ideals, it is perhaps because we have tried to be all things to all men: to run a school, an agronomic university, a retreat house, an old people's home, a shelter for delinquent boys and expectant mothers, a graduate school for the study of communities, of religions, of man and the state, of war and peace. We have aimed high; and we hope we have accomplished enough at least "to arouse the conscience." Here is the way – or rather here is *a* way – for those who love God and their neighbor to try to live by the two great commandments. The frustrations that we experience are exercises in faith and hope, which are supernatural virtues. With prayer, one can go on cheerfully and even happily, while without prayer, how grim is the journey. Prayer is as necessary to life as breathing. It is drink and food.

WE DO NOT ASK church or state for help, but we ask individuals, those who have subscribed to the *Catholic Worker* and so are evidently interested in what we are doing, presumably willing and able to help. Many a priest and bishop send help year after year. Somehow the dollars that come in cover current bills, help us to catch up with payments on back debts, and make it possible for us to keep on going. There is never anything left over, and we always have a few debts to keep us worrying, to make us more like the very poor we are trying to help. The wolf is not at the door, but he is trotting along beside us. We make friends with him, too, as Saint Francis did. We pray for the help we need, and it comes.

Once we overdrew our account by $200. On the way home from the printers, where we had been putting the paper to bed, we stopped in Chinatown at the little Church of the Transfiguration and said a prayer to Saint Joseph. When we got to the office a woman was waiting to visit with us. We served her tea and toast and presently she went on her way, leaving us a check for the exact amount of the overdraft. We had not mentioned our need.

What we pray for we receive.

POURING RAIN today. I stayed in, resting – feeling exhausted. Sorrow, grief, exhaust one. Then tonight the prayers, the rosaries I've been saying were answered. And the feeling that prayers are indeed answered when we cry out for help was a comfort in itself. I had the assurance that they were answered, though it might not be now.

I would not perhaps see the results. "Praised be God, the God of all consolation. He comforts us in all our afflictions and enables us to comfort those who are in trouble, with the same consolation we have had from him" (2 Cor. 1:3–4). Suffering draws us to prayer and we are comforted. Or at least strengthened to continue in faith, and hope, and love.

DESPITE MY FEELING of almost hopelessness and desperation, humanly speaking, I came through the day feeling singularly calm, peaceful, and happy.

Three conclusions were the result of my praying. First: My getting into a temper helped nobody. But remaining loving toward all helped to calm them all. Hence a great responsibility rests on me. Second: It was cruel to be harsh to anyone so absolutely dependent, as they are, humanly, on my kindness. Third: It is a healthy sign that they are not crushed and humbled toward other human beings by their own miseries. I mean, going around meekly for fear of me, or being humble out of human respect.

One must be humble only from a divine motive, otherwise humility is a debasing and repulsive attitude. To be humble and meek for love of God – that is beautiful. But to be humble and meek because your bread and butter depends on it is awful. It is to lose one's sense of human dignity.

Let reform come through love of God only, and from that love of God, love of each other. . . .

The aftereffects of last night's and this morning's heavy praying have been peace and joy and strength and thanksgiving, and a great deal of humility, too, at being so weak that God had to send me consolation to prepare me for the next trial.

I should know by this time that just because I *feel* that everything is useless and going to pieces and badly done and futile, it is not really that way at all. Everything is all right. It is in the hands of God. Let us abandon everything to Divine Providence.

O GOD, come to my assistance; O Lord, make haste to help us. Lord, hear my prayer, let my cry come to thee. In thee have I hoped, let me never be confounded. All I have on earth is thee. What do I desire in heaven beside thee?

And that "they" should have thee, find thee, love thee too, those you have given us, sent to us, our children, our flesh and blood. May they cry out for the living God. "No one comes to the Father but through me" (John 14:6). You have said this, Jesus. Draw them, I beg you, I plead with you, so that they "will run to the odor of your ointments" (Song of Sol. 1:3), that they will "taste and see that the Lord is sweet" (Ps. 34:8). Let them seek and find the way, the truth, the light.

9

Lord, Teach Me to Pray

Rejoice always, pray continually, give thanks in all circum-stances; for this is God's will for you in Christ Jesus.

I THESSALONIANS 5:16–18

I HAVE BEEN OVERCOME with grief at times, and felt my heart like a stone in my breast, it was so heavy, and always I have heard, too, that voice, "Pray."

What can we do? We can pray. We can pray without ceasing, as Saint Paul said. We can say with the apostles, "Lord, teach me to pray." We can say with Saint Paul, "Lord, what wilt thou have me to do?" (Acts 9:6). Will our Father give us a stone when we ask for bread?

We remember Jesus' words, "I tell you solemnly once again, if two of you on earth agree to ask anything at all, it will be granted to you by my Father in heaven. For where two or three meet in my name, I shall be there with them" (Matt. 18:19–20).

There is another bit of scripture which stands out in my mind these days. It is this: "Where sin abounded, there did grace more abound" (Rom. 5:20). Resting in this promise, I am content.

SO I RESOLVED then to be more careful not to omit certain devotions that I let myself off from on account of my irregular life and fatigue. After all, when I have been working from seven until twelve at night, or traveling fifteen hours by bus, I can realize all the more these words, "Can you not watch with me one hour?" (Matt 26:40). That, I have resolved, is to be my motto for the coming year, in order to foster recollection.

"Can you not watch with me one hour?"

I shall remember this whenever I am tired and want to omit prayer, the extra prayers I shall set myself. Because after all I am going to try to pray the simplest, humblest way, with no spiritual ambition.

Morning prayers, in my room before going to Mass. I always omit them, rushing out of the house just in time as I do. If I were less slothful it would be better. . . .

Around the middle of the day to take, even though it be to snatch, fifteen minutes of absolute quiet, thinking about God and talking to God.

The thing to remember is not to read so much or talk so much about God, but to talk to God.

To practice the presence of God.

MANY YOUNG PEOPLE have come here and worked with us, and they tell us after a while that they have learned a lot and are grateful to us, but they disagree with us on various matters – our pacifism, our opposition to the death penalty, our interest in small communities, and our opposition to the coercive power of the state. You people are impractical, they tell us, nice idealists, but not headed anywhere big and important. They are right. We *are* impractical, as one of us put it, as impractical as Calvary. There is no point in trying to make us into something we are not. We are *not* another community fund group, anxious to help people with some bread and butter and a cup of coffee or tea. We feed the hungry, yes; we try to shelter the homeless and give them clothes, if we have some, but there is a strong faith at work; we pray. If an outsider who comes to visit doesn't pay attention to our praying and what that means, then he'll miss the whole point of things.

During a visit to her daughter Tamar's growing family:

HOW TO LIFT THE HEART TO GOD, our first beginning and last end, except to say with the soldier about to go into battle – "Lord, I'll have no time to think of thee, but do thou think of me." Of course, there is grace at meals, a hasty grace, what with Sue trying to climb out of her high chair on the table. Becky used to fold her hands and look holy at the age of eighteen months, but now she does nothing. If you invite her participation, she says, "I won't." If you catch Sue in a quiet, un-hungry mood, she will be docile and fold her hands. But rarely. She is usually hungry, and when she starts to eat she starts to hum, which is thanks too.

But there is that lull in the morning before the mailman comes when I can take out the missal and read the epistle and gospel for the day. . . . That is refreshment always.

"The language of the Gospels, the style used by our Lord, leads us more directly to contemplation than the

technical language of the surest and loftiest theology,"
Garrigou-Lagrange* says. So this reading, directly from
the Gospels and the epistles of Saint Paul, is the best I
can have. The author of *The Cloud of the Unknowing***
talks of the conscious stretching out of the soul to God.
So I must try harder to pause even for a fraction of a
minute over and over again throughout the day, to reach
toward God.

NOW DON'T THINK that I've lost my mind – but I'll
tell you, I'll look at some of the cards I have, some of
Van Gogh's pictures of the poor, the coal miners, or
Daumier's, and I talk to those pictures! I look, and I
speak. I get strength from the way those writers and
artists portrayed the poor, that's how I've kept going all
these years. I pray to God and go visit him in churches;
and I have my conversational time with Van Gogh or
with Dickens – I mean, I'll look at a painting reproduced
on a postcard, that I use as a bookmark, or I read one
of those underlined pages in one of my old books, and
Lord, I've got my strength to get through the morning

* Réginald Garrigou-Lagrange, 1877–1964, French Catholic theologian
  and Dominican priest
** An anonymous work written in the late fourteenth century as a guide to
  contemplative prayer

or afternoon! When I die, I hope people will say that I tried to be mindful of what Jesus told us – his wonderful stories – and I tried my best to live up to his example (we fall flat on our faces all the time, though!) and I tried to take those artists and novelists to heart, and live up to *their* wisdom (a lot of it came from Jesus, as you probably know, because Dickens and Dostoyevsky and Tolstoy kept thinking of Jesus themselves all through their lives).

DRYNESS AND LACK OF RECOLLECTION can be good signs too, you know. God usually gives comfort to weak souls who need encouragement, and when they have progressed somewhat and he thinks they are strong enough to bear it, he permits this dryness. If you are faithful to your morning and evening prayers, and make your morning offering, and carry your rosary in your pocket so that you will remember to say even a part of it every day, you will be getting along fine. If you have to force yourself to pray, those prayers are of far more account with God than any prayers which bring comfort with them. That act of will is *very* important.

10

Give Thanks

Do not be anxious about anything, but in every situation, by prayer and petition, with thanksgiving, present your requests to God.

PHILIPPIANS 4:6

LATE THIS AFTERNOON the wind dropped and I sat by the open door contemplating the sunset. The waves lapped the shore, tingling among the shells and pebbles, and there was an acrid odor of smoke in the air. Down the beach the Belgians were working, loading rock into a small cart which looked like a tumbril, drawn by a bony white horse. They stooped as though in prayer, outlined against the brilliant sky, and as I watched, the bell from the chapel over at St. Joseph's rang the Angelus. I found myself praying, praying with thanksgiving, praying with open eyes, while I watched the workers on the beach, the sunset, and listened to the sound of the waves and the scream of snowy gulls.

"BUT," I REASONED with myself, "I am praying because I am happy, not because I am unhappy. I did not turn to God in unhappiness, in grief, in despair – to get consolation, to get something from him."

And encouraged that I was praying because I wanted to thank him, I went on praying. No matter how dull the day, how long the walk seemed, if I felt sluggish at the beginning of the walk, the words I had been saying insinuated themselves into my heart before I had finished, so that on the trip back I neither prayed nor thought but was filled with exultation.

IT IS CERTAINLY borne in upon us, day after day, how little it is that we do, or can do. But we are not alone. I remember that sense of shame at turning to God, as I lay in a cell at Occoquan, Virginia, so many years ago. I wanted to stand on my own feet. I thought there was something ignoble about calling for help in my despair, at my first taste of real destitution, of utter helplessness in the face of the vast sufferings of the world. I read the scriptures. . . . It was the only book we were allowed in jail. But I was ashamed and turned away in the pride of youth for another dozen years. Then it was in gratitude that I turned to him again, for my own happiness, for the beauty of the sea and the sand, for the smallest shell, the tiniest creature, the gulls, the sky and clouds. It is easier to praise God then, to thank him, to call upon him, and to learn that he does indeed answer.

But when we are able to bear some small share of the sufferings of the world, whether in pain of mind, body, or soul, let us thank God for that too. Maybe we are helping some prisoner, some Black or Puerto Rican youth in the Tombs,* some soldier in Vietnam. The old IWW** slogan "An injury to one is an injury to all" is another way of saying what Saint Paul said almost two thousand years ago. "We are all members of one another, and when the health of one member suffers, the health of the whole body is lowered." And the converse is true. We can indeed hold each other up in prayer. Excuse this preaching. I am preaching to myself too.

* An infamous city jail in Lower Manhattan
** Industrial Workers of the World, a revolutionary labor union

January and February are those months when winter seems interminable and vitality is low. In the face of world events, in the face of the mystery of suffering, of evil in the world, it is a good time to read the Book of Job, and then to go on reading the Psalms, looking for comfort – that is, strength to endure. Also to remember the importunate widow, the importunate friend. Both are stories which Jesus told. Then to pray without ceasing as Paul urged. And just as there was that interpolation in Job – that triumphant cry – "I know that my Redeemer liveth," so we, too, can know that help will come, that even from evil, God can bring great good, that indeed the good will triumph. Bitter though it is today with ice and sleet, the sap will soon be rising in those bare trees down the street from us.

A Way of Life

Jesus looked at him and loved him. "One thing you lack," he
said. "Go, sell everything you have and give to the poor, and
you will have treasure in heaven. Then come, follow me."

MARK 10:21

II

To Walk in His Way

He will teach us his ways, so that we may walk in his paths.

ISAIAH 2:3

From a letter to a friend when Dorothy was a high-school senior:

I'M STILL IN ACTS. I never went over it so thoroughly before and now I find much more in it. Isn't it queer how the same verses will strike you at different times? "We must through much tribulation enter into the kingdom of God." How true that is! Only after a hard bitter struggle with sin and only after we have overcome it, do we experience blessed joy and peace. The tears come to my eyes when I think how often I have gone through the bitter struggles and then succumbed to sin while peace was in sight. And after I fell how far away it fled. Poor weak creatures we are, yet God is our Father and God is love, ever present, ready to enfold us and comfort us and hold us up. . . . I know it seems foolish to try to be so Christlike – but God says we can – why else his command, "Be ye therefore perfect."

THE LONGER I LIVE, the more I see God at work in people who don't have the slightest interest in religion and never read the Bible and wouldn't know what to do if they were persuaded to go inside a church. I always knew how much I admired certain men and women (my "radical friends") who were giving their lives to help others get a better break; but now I realize how spiritual some of them were, and I'm ashamed of myself for not realizing that long ago, when I was with them, talking and having supper and making our plans, as we did.

BUT THERE IS NO POINT dwelling on the past excessively. My mother used to warn us against that; she'd say, "Doting on what's gone is wasting precious time." It's stealing time, really, from the present and from the future. If you believe in the mission of Jesus Christ, then you're bound to try to let go of your past, in the sense that you are entitled to his forgiveness. To keep regretting what was is to deny God's grace.

THE MAIN THING is never to get discouraged at the slowness of people or results. People may not be articulate or active, but even so, we do not ever know the results, or the effect on souls. That is not for us to know. We can only go ahead and work with happiness at what God sends us to do.

THE CHOICE is not between good and evil for Christians – it is not in this way that one proves his love. The very fact of baptism, of becoming a son of God, presupposes development as a son of God. C. S. Lewis, the author of *Screwtape Letters,* points out that the child in the mother's womb perhaps would refuse to be born if given the choice, but it does not have that choice. It has to be born. The egg has to develop into the chicken with wings. Otherwise it becomes a rotten egg. It is not between good and evil, I repeat, that the choice lies, but between good and better. In other words, we must give up over and over again even the good things of this world

to choose God. Mortal sin is a turning from God and a
turning to created things – created things that are good.

I HAVE COME to the conclusion that I have had so
much natural love in my life for people that God is now
proving me. He is pruning down my natural love so
that I may have more supernatural love. And the love
which comes out of this daily dying is real and true and
enduring. When I really learn to love, then all these contradictions will cease. I do truly realize that other people
see all my faults more clearly and they are quite rightly
irritated by me.

WE SHOULD HUNGER and thirst after holiness. Too
few even desire holiness. "Make us desire to walk in the
way of thy commandments" (Ps. 119:35).

Our lifelong fight as a Christian is to get off the
natural level and on the supernatural. Our lives must
be a pure act of love, repeated many times over. We are
invited to a life of infinitely higher level, union with
God. Baptistry a few steps down signifying burial, death
with Christ. We cultivate our human powers only as
they help us reach God. We have manhood, we are given
Christhood.

We always act out of motives – animal, human, or divine. There are three lives in us all seeking their loves. As long as we keep the lower subservient we have harmony. All day long we should keep on saying, "O my God, I love you," or "I am loving God."

Though we are given a share of divine life, we have no natural liking for it. Here is the source of all our difficulty and all our merit too.

OUR DESIRE FOR JUSTICE for ourselves and for others often complicates the issue, builds up factions and quarrels. Worldly justice and unworldly justice are quite different things. The supernatural approach when understood is to turn the other cheek, to give up what one has, willingly, gladly, with no spirit of martyrdom, to rejoice in being the least, to be unrecognized, the slighted.

FOR YEARS, in houses of hospitality around the country, speaking and writing and working, we have been trying to change the social order. Now these last years I realize that I must go further, go deeper, and work to make those means available for people to change themselves, so that they can change the social order. In order to have a Christian social order, we must first have

Christians. Father Lallemant* talks about how dangerous active work is without a long preparation of prayer.

GOING TO CONFESSION is hard. Writing a book
is hard, because you are "giving yourself away." But if
you love, you want to give yourself. You write as you
are impelled to write, about man and his problems, his
relation to God and his fellows. You write about yourself
because in the long run all man's problems are the same,
his human needs of sustenance and love. "What is
man that thou art mindful of him?" the Psalmist asks,
and he indicates man's immense dignity when he says,
"Thou hast made him a little less than the angels" (Ps.
8:4–5). He is made in the image and likeness of God;
he is a temple of the Holy Spirit. He is of tremendous
importance. What is man, where is he going, what is his
destiny? It is a mystery. We are sons of God, and "it is a
terrible thing to fall into the hands of the living God."

IT HAS ALWAYS SEEMED to me we are bound to have
an ebb and flow in our lives, like the tides. In Thomas à
Kempis's *The Imitation of Christ,* which I love and which
has always helped me in times of stress, it says some-
where that God's grace comes and goes, with no fault of

---

* Louis Lallemant, 1578–1635, French Jesuit

ours, and when we do not have it, we wait patiently and it returns. I do think manual labor of one kind or another is of help and when I get in states which last, I get to housecleaning, and there is always plenty of that around the Catholic Worker and farm, and that is some relief.

TO BE SIMPLE as little children, to live in the presence of God, to love God in his creatures, to do away with all suspicion, anger, contention and lack of brotherly love, to do the little things each day as well as we can and to start in all over again each morning, refreshing ourselves, steeling our wills – this is all we need to keep in mind.

I TRY TO THINK BACK; I try to remember this life that the Lord gave me; the other day I wrote down the words "a life remembered," and I was going to try to make a summary for myself, write what mattered most – but I couldn't do it. I just sat there and thought of our Lord, and his visit to us all those centuries ago, and I said to myself that my great luck was to have had him on my mind for so long in my life!

12

But How to Love?

I will give them an undivided heart and put a new spirit in them; I will remove from them their heart of stone and give them a heart of flesh.

EZEKIEL 11:19

MEN AND WOMEN have persisted in their hope for happiness. They have hoped against hope though all the evidence seemed to point to the fact that human nature could not be changed. Always they have tried to recover the lost Eden, and the history of our own country shows attempts to found communities where people could live together in that happiness which God seemed to have planned for us. . . .

Saint Teresa* said that you can only show your love for God by your love for your neighbor, for your brother and sister. Francois Mauriac, the novelist, and Jacques Maritain, the philosopher, said that when you were working for truth and justice you were working for Christ, even though you denied him.

But how to love? That is the question.

THE SOLUTION PROPOSED in the Gospels is that of voluntary poverty and the works of mercy. It is the little way. It is within the power of all. Everybody can begin here and now. . . . We have the greatest weapons in the world, greater than any hydrogen or atom bomb, and they are the weapons of poverty and prayer, fasting and alms, the reckless spending of ourselves in God's service and for his poor. Without poverty we will not have learned love, and love, at the end, is the measure by which we shall be judged.

AND NOW I PICK UP Thomas Merton's last book, *Contemplative Prayer,* which I am starting to read, and the foreword by our good Quaker friend Douglas Steere brought back to my memory a strange incident in my life. He quotes William Blake: "We are put on earth

* Teresa of Ávila, 1515–1582, Spanish mystic and Carmelite nun

for a little space that we may learn to bear the beams of love." And he goes on to say that to escape these beams, to protect ourselves from these beams, even devout men hasten to devise protective clothing. We do not want to be irradiated by love.

Suddenly I remembered coming home from a meeting in Brooklyn many years ago, sitting in an uncomfortable bus seat facing a few poor people. One of them, a downcast, ragged man, suddenly epitomized for me the desolation, the hopelessness of the destitute, and I began to weep. I had been struck by one of those "beams of love," wounded by it in a most particular way. It was my own condition that I was weeping about – my own hardness of heart, my own sinfulness. I recognized this as a moment of truth, an experience of what the *New Catechism* calls our "tremendous, universal, inevitable and yet inexcusable incapacity to love." I had not read that line when I had that experience, but that is what I felt. I think that ever since then I have prayed sincerely those scriptural verses, "Take away my heart of stone and give me a heart of flesh." I had been using this prayer as one of the three acts of faith, hope, and charity. "I believe, help thou my unbelief." "In thee have I hoped, let me never be confounded." "Take away my heart of stone and give me a heart of flesh," so that I may learn how to truly love my brother because in him, in his meanest guise, I am encountering Christ.

Perhaps I knew in that moment in the bus in Brooklyn what Saint Augustine meant when he cried out, "May I know myself so that I may know Thee." Because I felt so strongly my nothingness, my powerlessness to do anything about this horrifying recognition of my own hardness of heart, it drove me to the recognition that in God alone was my strength. Without him I could do nothing. Yet I could do all things in him who strengthened me. So there was happiness there, too. The tears were of joy as well as grief.

WHAT A PARADOX it is, this natural life and this supernatural life. We must give up our lives to gain them; we must die to live; we must be pruned to bear fruit. Ah yes, when we are being called appeasers, defeatists, we are being deprived of our dearest goods – our reputations, honor, the esteem of men – and we are truly on the way to becoming the despised of the earth. We are beginning perhaps to be truly poor.

We are trying to spread the gospel of peace, to persuade others to extend the peace movement, to build up a mighty army of conscientious objectors. And in doing this we are accounted fools, and it is the folly of the cross in the eyes of an unbelieving world.

Martyrdom is not gallantly standing before a firing squad. Usually it is the losing of a job because of not taking a loyalty oath, or buying a war bond, or paying a tax. Martyrdom is small, hidden, misunderstood. Or if it is a bloody martyrdom, it is the cry in the dark, the terror, the shame, the loneliness, nobody to hear, nobody to suffer with, let alone to save. Oh, the loneliness of all of us in these days, in all the great moments of our lives, this dying which we do, by little and by little, over a short space of time or over the years. One day is as a thousand in these crises. A week in jail is as a year.

But we repeat that we do see results from our personal experiences, and we proclaim our faith. Christ has died for us. Adam and Eve fell, and as Julian of Norwich wrote, the worst has already happened and been repaired. Christ continues to die in his martyrs all over the world, in his Mystical Body, and it is this dying, not the killing in wars, which will save the world.

Do we see results, do these methods succeed? Can we trust in them? Just as surely as we believe in "the little way" of Saint Therese,* we believe and know that this is the only success.

MUCH AS WE WANT TO, we do not really know ourselves. Do we really want to see ourselves as God sees us, or even as our fellow human beings see us? Could we bear it, weak as we are? . . . We do not want to be given that clear inward vision which discloses to us our most secret faults. In the Psalms there is that prayer "Deliver me from my secret sins" (Ps. 19:12). We do not really know how much pride and self-love we have until someone whom we respect or love suddenly turns against us. Then some sudden affront, some sudden offense we take, reveals to us in all its glaring distinctness our self-love, and we are ashamed.

WE ARE TOLD to put on Christ and we think of him in his private life, his life of work, his public life, his teaching and his suffering life. But we do not think enough of his life as a little child, as a baby. His helplessness, his powerlessness. We have to be content to be in that state too. Not to be able to do anything, to accomplish anything.

* Therese of Lisieux, 1873–1897, a French Discalced Carmelite nun who died at age twenty-four

ONE OF THE GREATEST EVILS of the day among those outside of prison is their sense of futility. Young people say, "What good can one person do? What is the sense of our small effort?" They cannot see that we must lay one brick at a time, take one step at a time; we can be responsible only for the one action of the present moment. But we can beg for an increase of love in our hearts that will vitalize and transform all our individual actions, and know that God will take them and multiply them, as Jesus multiplied the loaves and fishes.

CHARLES DE FOUCAULD* died a complete failure – no one followed him. He was killed in the desert in 1916. Rene Bazin wrote his life in 1922. Pere Voillaume read it in the seminary and in 1933 started his Little Brothers and now there are 600 of them, trusting to voluntary poverty, silence, prayer, the hidden life of Nazareth, and their spiritual influence is enormous. Who knows but that God will save the city with ten just men.

[A COWORKER] WROTE TO ME from the farm about that book, *In the Footsteps of St. Francis,* and recalled the danger of our becoming Brother Eliases instead of Saint

* Charles de Foucauld, 1858–1916, killed by bandits in Algeria, whose witness and writings inspired the founding of the Little Brothers of Jesus

Francises, in our order, efficiency, trying to get things done, etc. There is always that danger. We must contain ourselves in patience, remembering each morning that our main job is to love God and to serve him, and if we don't get things done due to interruptions, well, it cannot be helped, and God will take care of what we leave undone. But a tranquil spirit is important. Saint Teresa says that God cannot rest in an unquiet heart. I have to remember that many times during the day.

What if everything goes to rack and ruin? We can only do what we can to make order, but in the long run it's ourselves we have to look after.

I HAVE BEEN UPSET with myself on certain days; I wish I could just stay in my room and pray and read and ask God for his forgiveness. I know that when I go downstairs and talk to all the people there, and when I meet a lot of the people who come to visit us, and when I meet some of the people we serve – well (you may be offended if I say this), I might end up posing more than I would ever want to admit to myself at the time. It's only later that we stop and think about what we've been doing and how we might do better. Sometimes later is just a few hours afterward; sometimes later is weeks or months afterward, when everything has begun to blur, but there's a thorn inside you, and it won't stop giving you discomfort until you come clean. Peter [Maurin] used to say to me, "We can't expect to run to meet the world with our message and not fall flat on our faces. We've got to take the risk. We've got to get up after we fall and keep moving. If we say no, no more moving, because we made a mistake, made ten mistakes, a hundred, we're all washed up." And we must not be all washed up, he kept saying. (He liked that expression.) I would argue with him. I would tell him that if you keep stumbling and falling, it might be because you're doing something wrong. "Pray to God; ask for his help," he would answer. But then he'd add, "Keep moving, though." I guess we have.

*From a letter to Catherine de Hueck:**

YOU SOUNDED, TOO, so discouraged and you know as well as I do that discouragement is a temptation of the devil. Why should we try to see results? It is enough to keep on in the face of what looks to be defeat. We certainly have enough examples in the lives of the saints

---

* Catherine de Hueck Doherty, 1896–1985, founded Friendship House in Toronto in the early 1930s and Madonna House Apostolate in 1947. She shared many of Dorothy's concerns, and the two women encouraged each other in their attempts to live the gospel.

to help us. Not to speak of that greatest of failures (to the eyes of the world) of Christ on the cross. Why look for response? After all, we can only do what lies in our power and leave all the rest to God, and he will attend to it. You do not know yourself what you are doing, how far-reaching your influence is. I have heard people speak of you in different parts of the country. Why should you expect to see results in the shape of Houses of Friendship? Perhaps you are arousing in them instead the sense of personal responsibility. After all, God often lets us start doing one thing and many of the results we accomplish are incalculably far-reaching, splendid in their own way, but quite different from what we expected. Let us think only in terms of our own selves and God and not worry about anyone else.

I WAS THINKING, how as one gets older, we are tempted to sadness, knowing life as it is here on earth, the suffering, the cross. And how we must overcome it daily, growing in love, and the joy which goes with loving.

WHAT WITH BEING SICK this week, felt very low tonight. Read, prayed, wept, and then thought – why do we expect any happiness? God wills for us the present moment. We must take it with a joyful will at least. Never let our moods affect others. Hide any sadness. We are suffering sadness and fatigue just because our will is painfully struggling. Our Lord must teach me, I cannot learn by myself to give up my will completely, to accept the present moment, to live in the presence of God. I should be happy that this struggle is going on, that I am not content. A paradox. I was just reading over the last pages herein for my help. It serves to convince me that nothing depends on me, I can do nothing. Moods, discouragement, bickerings pass and the work proceeds, the influence is far-reaching.

MEDITATION ON THE BUS. Rainy and cold. Thinking gloomily of the sins and shortcomings of others, it suddenly came to me to remember my own offenses, just as heinous as those of others. If I concern myself with my own sins and lament them, if I remember my own failures and lapses, I will not be resentful of others. This was most cheering and lifted the load of gloom from my mind. It makes one unhappy to judge people and happy to love them.

I NEED SOME TIME ALONE for prayer and reading so that I can attain some proper perspective and peace of spirit to deal with myself and others. I need to overcome a sense of my own impotence, my own failure, and an impatience at others that goes with it. I must remember not to judge myself, as Saint Paul says. Such a sense of defeat comes from expecting too much of one's self, also from a sense of pride. More and more I realize how good God is to me to send me discouragements, failures, antagonisms.

The only way to proceed is to remember that God's ways are not our ways. To bear our own burdens, do our own work as best we can, and not fret because we cannot do more or do another's work. To be in that state of mind is to get nothing done.

ONE OF THE OBJECTIONS to suffering which we do not admit is that it is undignified. It is not a wound heroically received in battle. Hay fever, colds in the head, bilious attacks, poison ivy, such like irritations which are sometimes even worse than a severe illness are, to say the least, petty and undignified. But in reality it takes heroic virtue to practice patience in little things, things which seem little to others but which afflict one with unrest and misery. Patience with each other and with each other's bickerings. We can even offer up, however, our own lack of peace, our own worry. Since I offered all the distractions, turmoil, and unrest I felt at things going askew a few weeks ago, my petty fretting over this one and that one, I have felt much better and more able to cope with everything.

I SEEM ANGRY when I am silent very often just because of an expression of eye strain. All the more reason to speak gently. My problem is to try and be gentle and kind to *all*. Even, equable, never startling and saddening people by changes of mood. Lifting an atmosphere instead of lowering it. . . .

I have a hard enough job to curb the anger in my own heart which I sometimes even wake up with, go to sleep with – a giant to strive with, an ugliness, a sorrow to me – a mighty struggle to love. As long as there is any resentment, bitterness, lack of love in my own heart I am powerless. God must help me.

13

To Love Is to Suffer

Whoever wants to be my disciple must deny themselves and take up their cross and follow me.

MATTHEW 16:24

I DON'T only think of the Passion as the Crucifixion. I think of Jesus' whole life as "the Passion." I don't mean to become a theologian now; I have never been good at theology. My mind isn't abstract enough. But when I think of Jesus I think of someone who was *constantly* passionate; I think of all his experiences as part of his Passion: the stories he told, the miracles he performed, the sermons he delivered, the suffering he endured, the death he experienced. His whole life was a Passion – the energy, the love, the attention he gave to so many people, to friends and enemies alike.

CHRIST OUR LORD came and took upon himself our humanity. He became the Son of Man. He suffered hunger and thirst and hard toil and temptation. All power was his, but he wished the free love and service of men. He did not force anyone to believe. Saint Paul talks of the liberty of Christ. He did not coerce anyone. He emptied himself and became a servant. He showed the way to true leadership by coming to minister, not to be ministered unto. He set the example and we are supposed to imitate him. We are taught that his kingdom was not of this earth. He did not need pomp and circumstance to prove himself the Son of God.

His were hard sayings, so that even his own followers did not know what he was saying, did not understand him. It was not until after he died on the cross, it was not until he had suffered utter defeat, it would seem, and they thought their cause was lost entirely; it was not until they had persevered and prayed with all the fervor and desperation of their poor loving hearts, that they were enlightened by the Holy Spirit, and knew the truth with a strength that enabled them to suffer defeat and martyrdom in their turn. They knew then that not by force of arms, by the bullet or the ballot, would they conquer. They knew and were ready to suffer defeat – to show that great love which enabled them to lay down their lives for their friends.

WHEN WE SUFFER, we are told we suffer with Christ. We are "completing the sufferings of Christ." We suffer his loneliness and fear in the garden when his friends slept. We are bowed down with him under the weight of not only our own sins but the sins of each other, of the whole world. We are those who are sinned against and those who are sinning. We are identified with him, one with him. We are members of his Mystical Body.

THE ONLY ANSWER to this mystery of suffering is this: Every soul seeks happiness either in creatures (where it cannot be satisfied in the long run) or in God.

God made us for himself.

We must die to the natural to achieve the supernatural, a slow death or a quick one. It is universal. "Unless the grain of wheat fall into the ground and die, itself remaineth alone, but if it die, it beareth much fruit"

(John 12:24). All must die; it is a universal law very hard for us to realize.

If this mind or this flesh is an obstacle, we will suffer the more when this tremendous Lover tries to tear from us all veils which separate us. Some suffering is more visible, some hidden. If we long for beauty, the more our faith is tried, as though by fire, by ugliness. The more we long for love, the more all human love will be pruned, and the more we will see the venom of hatred about us. It is a pruning, a cutting away of love so that it will grow strong and bear much fruit. The more we long for power, the more we will destroy and tear down until we recognize our own weakness.

But still, suffering is a mystery as well as a penalty which we pay for others as well as for ourselves.

WHAT UNBEARABLE SUFFERING there is in the world today, all around us, in mental hospitals, in prisons as well as in war, and we know little more about them than the Germans claimed to know of the atrocities committed during the Holocaust in Europe. When we do know, what can we do? We cry out helplessly, to lighten the burden of suffering in the world. We have the teaching of Jesus on the works of mercy listed in the twenty-fifth chapter of Saint Matthew, of course.

I HAVE BEEN VISITING FAMILIES all along the way, and there are many tragedies in our midst. While I was in Mexico I talked with a saintly old priest, eighty, and all he talked about was the need for suffering, the joy in suffering, and how we had to bear our share, and I just burst into tears, and I told him I found it very hard to take, just to think of all the suffering that might happen to Tamar and the family, for instance. He comforted me by saying God never asked anything of you that he did not give you beforehand. But we sure have to bear our part, each one of us in one form or another. If we could only learn to relax under it. If we could only learn that the only important thing is love, and that we will be judged on love – to keep on loving, and showing that love, and expressing that love, over and over, whether we feel it or not, seventy times seven, to mothers-in-law, to husbands, to children – and to be oblivious of insult, or hurt, or injury – not to see them, not to hear them. It is a hard, hard doctrine. I guess we get what we need in the way of discipline. God can change things in a twinkling of an eye. We have got to pray, to read the gospel, to get to frequent communion, and not judge, not do anything but love, love, love. A bitter lesson. Where there is no love, put love and you will take out love, Saint John of the Cross* says.

HOW TO DRAW A PICTURE of the strength of love! It seems at times that we need a blind faith to believe in it at all. There is so much failure all about us. It is so hard to reconcile oneself to such suffering, such long, enduring suffering of body and soul, that the only thing one can do is to stand by and save the dying ones who have given up hope of reaching out for beauty, joy, ease, and pleasure in this life. For all their reaching, they got little of it. To see these things in the light of faith, God's mercy, God's justice! His devouring love!

HOW SUFFERING drives us to prayer! I mean mental suffering, caused by the sin of those you love. But it seems that to love is to suffer. One must constantly recall the necessity to grow in confidence in God. The word means "with faith." *Con fide.* An opportunity then to grow in faith. Confidence, trust, trust in one another too. Trust that prayers will be answered. Maybe not as we want but as others need it to be.

* John of the Cross, 1542–1591, a Spanish mystic and Carmelite friar

TO LOVE IS TO SUFFER. Perhaps our only assurance that we do love God, Jesus, is to accept this suffering joyfully! What a contradiction!

IF IT WERE NOT FOR SCRIPTURE on the one hand and communion on the other, I could not bear my life, but daily it brings me joy in this sorrow which is part of our human condition, and a real, very real and vital sense of the meaning and the fruitfulness of these sufferings. Thomas à Kempis, a mystic not at all in fashion now, says that in the cross is joy of spirit. Jesus said, "Take up your cross and follow me." There is no one living who is not bearing a cross of some kind, and if the crosses of others look to you to be unbearable, so that you find yourself suffering for them as well as for yourself, then I am lacking in faith. "My grace is sufficient," God promises us.

COMPASSION – it is a word meaning "to suffer with." If we all carry a little of the burden, it will be lightened. If we share in the suffering of the world, then some will not have to endure so heavy an affliction. It evens out. What you do here in New York, in Harrisburg, helps those in China, India, South Africa, Europe, and Russia, as well as in the oasis where you are. You may think you are alone. But we are members one of another. We are children of God together.

I WRITE TO COMFORT OTHERS as I have been comforted. The word *comfort* too means to be strong together, to have fortitude together. There is the reminder of community. Once when I suffered and sat in church in a misery while waves and billows passed over me, I suddenly thought, with exultation, "I am sharing suffering," and it was immediately lightened.

IN PATIENCE you will possess your souls. Patience means suffering and suffering is spiritual work, and it is accomplishing something though we don't realize it until later. It is a part of our education, or pilgrimage to heaven. By it we keep in mind that all the way to heaven is heaven. Heaven is within you. The kingdom is here and now.

So joy and suffering go together, pleasure and pain, work and rest, the rhythm of life, day succeeding the night, spring following winter, life and death and life again, world without end.

14

Glory and Beauty

I will be glad and rejoice in you; I will sing the praises of your name, O Most High.

PSALM 9:2

ON THE ONE HAND, there is the sadness of the world – and on the other hand, when I went to church today and the place was flooded with sunshine, and it was a clear, cold day outside . . . suddenly my heart was so flooded with joy and thankfulness and so overwhelmed at the beauty and the glory and the majesty of our God.

When Dorothy was fifteen:

HOW I LOVE THE PARK in winter! So solitary and awful in the truest meaning of the word. God is there. Of course, he is everywhere, but under the trees and looking over the wide expanse of lake he communicates himself to me and fills me with a deep quiet peace. I need those hours alone in the afternoon with the baby *[her younger brother John]* and I feel as though the troubles of life are lifted until I return to the houses and it all comes back to me.

MASS AT EIGHT. Most beautiful surroundings. Low tide and I collected shells, very large mussels.

Two "lights" which came to me in my life for which I shall be always thankful. One at sixteen: that I could earn a living by manual labor, housework, and so honorably could obtain my bread. I failed to remember this when I asked Saint Anthony to send me a job writing!

Second light at twenty-six when I realized that the pleasures of the intellect would grow, that the delights in the search for God would never end – at the beach.

ONE LINE of a psalm is: "Be still and know that I am God" (Ps. 46:10). You hear things in your own silences.

The beauty of nature, including the sound of waves, the sound of insects, the cicadas in the trees – all were part of my joy in nature that brought me to the church. I don't think we can overemphasize the importance of song. Psalm 96 begins: "Sing to the Lord a new song. . . . Sing joyfully to the Lord, all you lands; break into song; sing praise. . . . Let the sea and what fills it resound, the world and those who dwell in it. Let the rivers clap their hands, the mountains shout with them for joy."

I OWE GREAT THANKS to God that he gave me an appreciation of his beauty so young. Certainly I thank my father who always saw to it that we lived as near as possible to a park or beach, in all our wanderings around the country. I remember the beach when we lived in what is now known as the Bay Ridge section of Brooklyn. I went there with my two older brothers and I went there alone even before I went to school. I walked through the swamp near Fort Hamilton and remember the enormously tall grasses and the path we made through them to the rivulet where we caught eels.

I have never gotten over my love for the sound of water, little waves lapping on the beach, retreating through the heaps of small stones and shells. On other days there was the strong sound of breakers pounding on the beach and the smell of the salt spray. I remember the taste of the seeds I nibbled, the hearts of the thistle burrs which we ate, and the taste too of salt from the shells and stones which like little animals we liked to lick. All senses were engaged: sight, sound, smell, taste, and, yes, touch, because the feel of things gave us sensuous delight.

I am sure that it is because the church is so alert to man, as body and soul, because she believes in the resurrection of the body and life everlasting, that I became strongly attracted to her when I began to catch glimpses of her later.

THIS MONTH OF THANKSGIVING will indeed be one of gratitude to God. For health, for work to do, for the opportunities he has given us of service; we are deeply grateful, and it is a feeling that makes the heart swell with joy.

During the summer when things were going especially hard in more ways than one, I grimly modified grace before meals: "We give thee thanks, O Lord, for these thy gifts, and for all our tribulations, from thy bounty, through Christ our Lord, Amen." One could know of certain knowledge that tribulations were matters of thanksgiving; that we were indeed privileged to share in the sufferings of Our Lord. So in this month of thanksgiving, we can be thankful for the trials of the past, the blessings of the present, and be heartily ready at the same time to embrace with joy any troubles the future may bring us.

BOOKS [TO READ] IN WARTIME: *Labyrinthine Ways. To the End of the World. Kristin Lavransdatter. Master of Hestviken.* Jeremiah. 1 Kings.

People live, eat, sleep, love, worship, marry, have children, and somehow live in the midst of war, in the midst of anguish. The sun continues to shine, the leaves flaunt their vivid color, there is a serene warmth in the day and an invigorating cold at night.

Turn off your radio. Put away your daily paper. Read one review of events a week and spend some time reading such books as the above. They tell too of days of striving and of strife. They are of other centuries and also of our own. They make us realize that all times are perilous, that men live in a dangerous world, in peril constantly of losing or maiming soul and body.

We get some sense of perspective reading such books. Renewed courage and faith and even joy to live. And

man cannot live long without joy, without some vestige
of happiness to light up his days.

As a child, Dorothy attended Sunday services in an
Episcopal church, where she learned the Psalms and hymns
that would stay with her for life.

THE SONG thrilled in my heart, and though I was only
ten years old, through these Psalms and canticles I called
on all creation to join with me in blessing the Lord. I
thanked him for creating me, saving me from all evils,
filling me with all good things.

Whenever I felt the beauty of the world in song or
story, in the material universe around me, or glimpsed it
in human love, I wanted to cry out with joy. The Psalms
were an outlet for this enthusiasm of joy or grief – and
I suppose my writing was also an outlet. After all, one
must communicate ideas. I always felt the common unity
of our humanity; the longing of the human heart is for
this communion. If only I could sing, I thought, I would
shout before the Lord, and call upon the world to shout
with me, "All ye works of the Lord, bless ye the Lord,
praise him and glorify him forever." My idea of heaven
became one of fields and meadows, sweet with flowers
and songs and melodies unutterable, in which even the

laughing gull and the waves on the shore would play their part.

ONE THING I KEPT THINKING OF when I was in jail [five days for civil disobedience]: Fr. Hugo's ministry in Pittsburgh, as chaplain of the workhouse and the city jail. I have heard that he begs for the choirs in the city to sing the Mass for the prisoners. "A prayer sung is twice said," Saint Augustine wrote. So there in prison great praise, honor, and glory is offered to God, great thanksgiving, great supplication for the poor and for sinners.

THIS MORNING AT SIX I was reading Saint John's Passion, and when Jesus was brought before Pilate, he was "asked about his disciples and his doctrine."

He certainly answered nothing about his disciples – he just said he had been preaching openly.

Our lives are open to all. We belong to a kingdom not of this world, though we are in it. May you be a constant reminder, a witness, of this other kingdom, this glorious and beautiful kingdom where we are willing and obedient and joyful subjects.

WE WANT TO BE HAPPY, we want others to be happy, we want to see some of this joy of life which children have, we want to see people intoxicated with God, or just filled with the good steady joy of knowing that Christ is king and that we are his flock and he has prepared for us a kingdom, and that God loves us as a father loves his children, as a bridegroom loves his bride, and that eye hath not seen nor ear heard what God hath prepared for us!

A Way of Community

Whoever does the will of my Father in heaven is my brother and sister and mother.

MATTHEW 12:50

15

Seeing Christ
in All Who Come

Truly I tell you, whatever you did for one of the least of these brothers and sisters of mine, you did for me.

MATTHEW 25:40

DO WE GET MUCH HELP from Catholic Charities? We are often asked this question. I can say only that it is not the church or the state to which we turn when we ask for help in these appeals. Cardinal Spellman did not ask us to undertake this work, nor did the Mayor of New York. It just happened. It is the living from day to day, taking no thought for the morrow, seeing Christ in all who come to us, trying literally to follow the gospel, that resulted in this work.

"Give to him that asketh of thee, and from him that would borrow of thee turn not away. . . . Love your enemies; do good to those who hate you, pray for those who persecute and calumniate you" (Matt. 5:42, 44).

LAST WEEK a woman came in with a policeman. She was a very difficult alcoholic whom Irene, who has charge of the women's house, had tried to help for the past six months. Over and over again she had cleaned Ann up, had tried to get her on her feet, had helped her to jobs, had forgiven her seventy times seven rather than put her out on the streets. The last time she was drunk, she had lost ten dollars in the house and we found it. Tom has charge of the money of the house, and it was turned over to him and used for "flop money" for others, for beans for the soup, or whatnot. When she next came in, sober, with a job, and asked for her money, we told her that we had found it but used it. We live often from day to day, so there was nothing at that moment in the house to give her. We did not say that she owed us far more for her six months' stay with us. And now here she was, coming in threateningly with a policeman, demanding we give her the ten dollars.

"Give her your cloak, too," Bob said.

How to love! How to turn the other cheek, how to give your cloak and your trousers and your shoes, and then when you are left naked, you are beaten and reviled besides. . . .

There was a sense of relief that she was gone, that she had met her match, that a difficult situation had been handled, but not by us – that she had been gotten rid of. But where has she gone? She is one of our many failures.

FAILURES. It is these things that overwhelm one. Physical sickness like epilepsy, senility, insanity, drug cases, alcoholics; and just the plain, ordinary poor who can't get along, can't find a place to live, who need clothes, shelter, food, jobs, care, and most of all love – these are the daily encounters. . . .

How can we ever give up thinking and longing for love, talking of it, preparing ourselves for it, reading of it, studying about it? It is really a great faith in love that never dies. We hope against hope, as Abraham did in the promise, and we know with something that bears witness in us that this love is true, and that the promise is there.

I am speaking of heavenly things, but heaven and earth are linked together as the body and soul are linked together. We begin to live again each morning. We rise from the dead, the sun rises, spring comes around – there is always that cycle of birth and growth and death, and then resurrection.

LET US REJOICE in poverty, because Christ was poor. Let us love to live with the poor, because they are specially loved by Christ. Even the lowest, most depraved – we must see Christ in them and love them to folly. When we suffer from dirt, lack of privacy, heat and cold, coarse food, let us rejoice.

When we are weary of manual labor and think, "What foolishness to shovel out ashes, build fires, when we can have steam heat! Why sew when it can be better done on a machine? Why laboriously bake bread when we can buy so cheaply?" Such thoughts have deprived us of good manual labor in our city slums and have substituted shoddy store-bought goods, clothes, and bread.

Poverty and manual labor – they go together. They are weapons of the spirit, and very practical ones too. What would one think of a woman who refused to wash her clothes because she had no washing machine, or clean her house because she had no vacuum, or sew because she had no machine? In spite of the usefulness of the machine, and we are not denying it, there is still much to be done by hand. So much, one might say, that it is useless to multiply our tasks, go in for work for work's sake.

But we must believe in it for Christ's sake. We must believe in poverty and manual labor for love of Christ and for love of the poor. It is not true love if we do not know them, and we can only know them by living with them, and if we love with knowledge we will love with faith, hope, and charity.

16

Living Together, Working Together

No one who has left home or brothers or sisters or mother or father or children or fields for me and the gospel will fail to receive a hundred times as much in this present age: homes, brothers, sisters, mothers, children and fields – along with persecutions – and in the age to come, eternal life.

MARK 10:29–30

THE ONLY ANSWER in this life, to the loneliness we are all bound to feel, is community. The living together, working together, sharing together, loving God and loving our brother, and living close to him in community so we can show our love for Him.

WHENEVER I GROAN within myself and think how hard it is to keep writing about love in these times of tension and strife, which may at any moment become for us all a time of terror, I think to myself, "What else is the world interested in?" What else do we all want, each one of us, except to love and be loved, in our families, in our work, in all our relationships? God is love. Love casts out fear. Even the most ardent revolutionist, seeking to change the world, to overturn the tables of the money changers, is trying to make a world where it is easier for people to love, to stand in that relationship to each other. We want with all our hearts to love, to be loved. And not just in the family but to look upon all as our mothers, sisters, brothers, children. It is when we love the most intensely and most humanly that we can recognize how tepid is our love for others. The keenness and intensity of love brings with it suffering, of course, but joy too, because it is a foretaste of heaven.

Dorothy recalls experiencing community as a young child:

WE WERE IN CALIFORNIA until after the earthquake which shook us eastward. We were living in Oakland at the time, and though I remember some years later praying fearfully during a lightning storm, I do not remember praying during that cataclysmic disturbance, the earthquake.

What I remember most plainly about the earthquake was the human warmth and kindliness of everyone afterward. For days, refugees poured out of burning San Francisco and camped in Idora Park and the racetrack in Oakland. People came in their nightclothes; there were newborn babies.

Mother had always complained before about how clannish California people were, how if you were from the East they snubbed you and were loath to make friends. But after the earthquake everyone's heart was enlarged by Christian charity. All the hard crust of worldly reserve and prudence was shed. Each person was a little child in friendliness and warmth.

Mother and all our neighbors were busy from morning to night cooking hot meals. They gave away every extra garment they possessed. They stripped themselves to the bone in giving, forgetful of the morrow. While the crisis lasted, people loved each other. They realized their own helplessness while nature "travaileth and groaneth." It was as though they were united in Christian solidarity. It makes one think of how people could, if they would, care for each other in times of stress, unjudgingly, with pity and with love.

CHILDREN LOOK AT THINGS very directly and simply. I did not see anyone taking off his coat and giving it to the poor. I didn't see anyone having a banquet and calling in the lame, the halt, and the blind. And those who were doing it, like the Salvation Army, did not appeal to me. I wanted, though I did not know it then, a synthesis. I wanted life and I wanted the abundant life. I wanted it for others too. I did not want just the few, the missionary-minded people like the Salvation Army, to be kind to the poor, as the poor. I wanted everyone to be kind. I wanted every home to be open to the lame, the halt, and the blind, the way it had been after the San Francisco earthquake. Only then did people really live, really love their brothers. In such love was the abundant life and I did not have the slightest idea how to find it.

PETER MAURIN,* founder of a movement, a man of vision, changing the course of thought of thousands, has talked for fifteen years of crafts, of manual labor. Yet how many have tried to acquire a skill, either to carpenter, lay brick, make shoes, tailor, or work at a forge? Many, thinking of the family, the need for a home and space and food, have turned to the farm. But a farmer needs capital and many skills, besides the *habit of work*. Village economy could use doctors, barbers, veterinarians, bakers, launderers, canners, builders, shoemakers, tailors, etc. Not to speak of weavers. Every man, doing some particular job, could be an artist too, and from his work, beauty would overflow.

A PHILOSOPHY OF WORK is essential if we would be whole men, holy men, healthy men, joyous men. A certain amount of goods is necessary for a man to lead a good life, and we have to make that kind of society where it is easier for men to be good. These are all things Peter

---

* Peter Maurin, 1877–1949, born Pierre Aristide Maurin in France, cofounded the Catholic Worker movement. Dorothy Day wrote, "When people come into contact with Peter they change, they awaken, they begin to see, things become as new, they look at life in the light of the Gospels. They admit the truth he possesses and lives by, and though they themselves fail to go the whole way, their faces are turned at least towards the light." (*Peter Maurin: Apostle to the World,* by Dorothy Day).

Maurin wrote about. . . .

A philosophy of work and a philosophy of poverty are necessary if we would share with all men what we have, if we would each try to be the least, if we would wash the feet of our brothers. It is necessary if we would so choose to love our brother, live for him and die for him, rather than kill him in war.

PETER'S PLAN was that groups should borrow from mutual-aid credit unions in the parish to start what he first liked to call agronomic universities, where the worker could become a scholar and the scholar a worker. Or he wanted people to give the land and money. He always spoke of giving. Those who had land and tools should give. "Love is an exchange of gifts," Saint Ignatius had said. It was in these simple, practical, down-to-earth ways that people could show their love for each other. If the love was not there in the beginning, but only the need, such gifts made love grow.

COMMUNITY – that was the social answer to the long loneliness. That was one of the attractions of religious life, and why couldn't lay people share in it? Not just the basic community of the family, but also a community of families, with a combination of private and communal property. This could be a farming commune, a continuation of the agronomic university Peter spoke of as a part of the program we were to work for. Peter had vision and we all delighted in these ideas.

I STILL THINK that the only solution is the land, and *community,* a community which is unjudging and which forgives "seventy times seven," as Jesus Christ said. We who think in terms of community at least have the assurance, the conviction, that we are on the right path, going in the right direction, taking the right means to achieve the goal of increased love of God through an increased and proven love of our brothers. So many in these days have taken violent steps to gain the things of this world – war to achieve peace; coercion to achieve freedom; striving to gain what slips through the fingers. We might as well give up our great desires, at least our hopes of doing great things toward achieving them, right at the beginning. In a way it is like that paradox of the gospel, of giving up one's life in order to save it.

I THINK OF YOU ALL so often. . . . How I hope you can get a bigger house so you can have discussion groups, a library, a guest room, a Christ room, etc. – all that will go to make a Christian community. The first and greatest of all communities is the *home*; if things are not right there nothing can make them right.

WE MUST PRACTICE the presence of God. He said that when two or three are gathered together, there he is in the midst of them. He is with us in our kitchens, at our tables, on our breadlines, with our visitors, on our farms. When we pray for our material needs, it brings us close to his humanity. He, too, needed food and shelter; he, too, warmed his hands at a fire and lay down in a boat to sleep.

17

A Place Where Love Can Grow

Endure hardship as discipline; God is treating you as his children. For what children are not disciplined by their father?

HEBREWS 12:7

Here Dorothy writes to a nineteen-year-old coworker left responsible for publishing the newspaper while Dorothy was traveling:

DO NOT BE AFRAID of being the least, and doing the little things around the place. Look how Peter [Maurin] works, how he is always looking for things that he can do. Please do try to be as industrious as possible and if you are leaving the office late in the evening, set an example by cleaning up the two offices before you go. Even though you are only around a couple of nights a week, it makes a difference, and we cannot stress too much this idea of personal responsibility (paying no attention to what the other fellow does or does not do) but doing everything we see to do ourselves. After all, we are doing it first of all for God, and then for each other.

To another coworker she wrote:

IT IS IMPORTANT that we try to stick together and be loyal to each other and try to see each other's good points. God knows, living together we can see each other's bad points and weaknesses quick enough. We can be under no delusions. But we can never have enough mutual love.

I know I can trust you to see that visitors are properly taken care of, that people are treated with consideration. I know you sometimes get impatient, but I know, too, that you are sorry for it.

SAINT JOHN THE BAPTIST, when asked what was to be done, said "He that hath two coats let him give to him who hath none." And we must ask for greater things than immediate necessities. I believe that we should ask the rich to help the poor, as Vinoba Bhave* does in India, but this is hard to do; we can only make it easier by practice. "Let your abundance supply their want," Saint Paul says.

Easiest of all is to have so little, to have given away so much, that there is nothing left to give. But is this ever true? This point of view leads to endless discussions, but the principle remains the same. We *are* our brother's keeper. Whatever we have beyond our own needs belongs to the poor. If we sow sparingly, we will reap sparingly. And it is sad but true that we must give far more than bread, than shelter.

If you are the weaker one in substance, in mental or physical health, then you must receive, too, with humility and a sense of brotherhood. I always admired that simplicity of Alyosha in *The Brothers Karamazov* which led him to accept quite simply the support he needed from the benefactors who took him in.

If we do give in this way, then the increase comes. There will be enough. Somehow we will survive; "The pot of meal shall not waste, nor the cruze of oil be

---

* Vinayak Narahari "Vinoba" Bhave, 1895–1982, Indian advocate of non-violence and human rights

diminished" (1 Kings 17:14), for all our giving away the last bit of substance we have.

At the same time we must often be settling down happily to the cornmeal cakes, the last bit of food in the house, before the miracle of the increase comes about. Any large family knows these things – that somehow everything works out. It works out naturally and it works out religiously.

TRUE LOVE IS DELICATE and kind, full of gentle perception and understanding, full of beauty and grace, full of joy unutterable. "Eye hath not seen, nor ear heard . . . what God hath prepared for those who love him" (1 Cor. 2:9).

And there should be some flavor of this in all our love for others. We are all one. We are one flesh in the Mystical Body, as man and woman are said to be one flesh in marriage. With such a love one would see all things new; we would begin to see people as they really are, as God sees them.

We may be living in a desert when it comes to such perceptions now, and that desert may stretch out before us for years. But a thousand years are as one day in the sight of God, and soon we will know as we are known.

Until then, we will have glimpses of brotherhood in play, in suffering, in serving, and we will begin to train for that community.

A COMMUNITY is not a place where "desert fathers" are testing themselves – more and more, harder and harder, each on his own. A community is what Saint Paul told us – our differences granted respect by one another, but those differences are not allowed to turn us into loners. You must know when to find your own, quiet moment of solitude. But you must know when to open the door to go be with others, and you must know *how* to open the door. There's no point in opening the door with bitterness and resentment in your heart. I have noticed that those alcoholics, those bums and tramps and ne'er-do-wells have a way of reading our faces, getting quickly to the truth of our souls. They do that, I fear, better than we do with one another. We try to protect one another, we "cover" for one another – oh, maybe we don't want to see in each other what we don't want to see in the privacy of our own rooms staring into the mirror: our sins at work in our lives.

I remember one day realizing that the best, the very best, I could do for everyone in the community, including our guests at lunch, was to stay away, not to fight staying away, which I might have done successfully. There are times when one's generosity is a mask for one's pride: what will "they" do without me, without my energy put at their disposal?

YOUTH DEMANDS THE HEROIC, Claudel* said, and youth likes to dream of heroic deeds and of firing squads, of martyrs and of high adventure. But bread means life too; and money, which buys bread, for which we work, also means life. Sharing and community living mean laying down your life for your fellows also. . . .

We have repeated so many times that those who have two cloaks should follow the early Fathers, who said, "The coat that hangs in your closet belongs to the poor." And those who have a ten-room house can well share it with those who have none and who are forced to live in a municipal lodging house. How many large houses could be made into several apartments to take in others? Much hospitality could be given to relieve the grave suffering today. But people are afraid. They do not know where it all will end. They have all gone far enough in generosity to know that an ordeal is ahead, that the person taken

* Paul Claudel, 1868–1955, French poet, dramatist, and diplomat

in will turn into "the friend of the family," most likely, or "the man who came to dinner." No use starting something that you cannot finish, they say. Once bitten is twice shy. We have all had our experiences of ingratitude, of nursing a viper in our bosom, as the saying goes. So we forget about pruning in the natural order in order to attain much fruit. We don't want to pay the cost of love. We do not want to exercise our capacity to love.

WE SUFFER THESE THINGS and they fade from memory. But daily, hourly, to give up our own possessions and especially to subordinate our own impulses and wishes to others – these are hard, hard things; and I don't think they ever get any easier.

You can strip yourself, you can be stripped, but still you will reach out like an octopus to seek your own comfort, your untroubled time, your ease, your refreshment. It may mean books or music – the gratification of the inner senses – or it may mean food and drink, coffee and cigarettes. The one kind of giving up is no easier than the other.

Occasionally – often after reading the life of such a saint as Benedict Joseph Labre* – we start thinking about

---

* Benedict Joseph Labre, 1748–1783, a French mendicant belonging to the Third Order of Saint Francis

poverty, about going out alone, living with the destitute, sleeping on park benches or in the city shelter, living in churches, sitting before the Blessed Sacrament as we see so many doing who come from the municipal lodging house or the Salvation Army around the corner. And when such thoughts come on warm spring days, when children are playing in the park and it is good to be out on the city streets, we know that we are only deceiving ourselves: for we are only dreaming of a form of luxury. What we want is the warm sun, and rest, and time to think and read, and freedom from the people who press in on us from early morning until late at night. No, it is not simple, this business of poverty.

Over and over again in the history of the church the saints have emphasized voluntary poverty. Every religious community, begun in poverty and incredible hardship, but with a joyful acceptance of hardship by the rank-and-file priests, brothers, monks, or nuns who gave their youth and energy to good works, soon began to "thrive." Property was extended until holdings and buildings accumulated; and, although there is still individual poverty in the community, there is corporate wealth. It is hard to remain poor.

WE ARE COMMUNITIES in time and in a place, I know, but we are communities in faith as well – and sometimes time can stop shadowing us. Our lives are touched by those who lived centuries ago, and we hope that our lives will mean something to people who won't be alive until centuries from now. It's a great "chain of being," someone once told me, and I think our job is to do the best we can to hold up our small segment of the chain. That's one kind of localism, I guess, and one kind of politics – doing your utmost to keep that chain connected, unbroken. Our arms are linked – we try to be neighbors of His, and to speak up for his principles. That's a lifetime's job.

WE CANNOT LOVE GOD unless we love each other, and to love we must know each other. We know him in the breaking of bread, and we know each other in the breaking of bread, and we are not alone any more. Heaven is a banquet and life is a banquet, too, even with a crust, where there is companionship.

We have all known the long loneliness and we have learned that the only solution is love and that love comes with community.

Notes

A Way of Faith

Chapter 1

3 I remember the first radio   *The Duty of Delight,* 612

4 The ceremony of baptism   *On Pilgrimage,* 108

5 I believed in Jesus Christ   *Dorothy Day: A Radical Devotion,* 55

Faith came before   *All the Way to Heaven,* 271

You are certainly going   *All the Way to Heaven,* 429

6 Life would be utterly unbearable   *From Union Square to Rome,* 119

Faith, more precious   *The Duty of Delight,* 388–89

7 It is the First Letter of Peter   *All the Way to Heaven,* 498

Chapter 2

8 Faith is required   *By Little and by Little,* 171

9 Without faith   *The Long Loneliness,* 256

10 These hot August days   *The Duty of Delight,* 133

We may be living   *On Pilgrimage,* 85

The first job   *The Duty of Delight,* 339

11 To grow in faith   *The Duty of Delight,* 540

12 I have had so many years   *All the Way to Heaven,* 449

Chapter 3

13 Without the sacraments   *The Duty of Delight,* 519

14 Do what comes   *House of Hospitality,* 114, 118

15 In a way your letter   *All the Way to Heaven,* 330

This morning   *All the Way to Heaven,* 317–18

16 Today the atmosphere   *The Duty of Delight,* 351

We know how powerless   *All the Way to Heaven,* 470

One time I was traveling   *On Pilgrimage,* 197

Chapter 4

18 The grace of hope   *The Catholic Worker,* May 1978

19 I have fallen in love   *The Duty of Delight,* 488–89

20 Hope and faith   *The Duty of Delight,* 520

21 Life gets harder   *The Duty of Delight,* 546

A Way of Love

Chapter 5

25 There is a character   *On Pilgrimage,* 233

26 Love and ever more love   *House of Hospitality,* 267

27 In Christ's human life   *The Catholic Worker,* December 1945

28 Jesus Christ knew   *On Pilgrimage,* 204

29 My soul hath thirsted   *On Pilgrimage,* 243

Chapter 6

31 How much did I hear   *The Long Loneliness,* 12

32 But always the glimpses   *From Union Square to Rome,* 10
     Our prayer should be   *On Pilgrimage,* 190–91

33 Our greatest danger   *On Pilgrimage,* 191
     All other loves   *On Pilgrimage,* 192

34 Two people   *On Pilgrimage,* 192
     Results?   *On Pilgrimage,* 196

35 When we are asked   *All the Way to Heaven,* 427
     Eye hath not seen   *The Duty of Delight,* 386

36 I am convinced   *All the Way to Heaven,* 471

Chapter 7

37 I am terribly afraid   *All the Way to Heaven,* 419

38 There are all kinds   *The Catholic Worker,* February 1960
     Do you remember   *From Union Square to Rome,* 8

39 Woke up this a.m.   *The Duty of Delight,* 395
     What is God   *On Pilgrimage,* 233–34

40 The love of God   *On Pilgrimage,* 235

Love must be tried   *On Pilgrimage,* 238

A Way of Prayer

Chapter 8

43 Does God have a set way   *Dorothy Day: A Radical Devotion,* 28

Being on one's knees   *The Duty of Delight,* 42

44 I do believe in a personal God   *The Duty of Delight,* 507–8

If we have failed to achieve   *Loaves and Fishes,* 206

45 We do not ask church or state   *Loaves and Fishes,* 91

46 Pouring rain today   *The Duty of Delight,* 533

47 Despite my feeling   *House of Hospitality,* 133

48 O God, come to my assistance   *The Duty of Delight,* 532–33

Chapter 9

49 I have been overcome with grief   *By Little and by Little,* 184

50 So I resolved then   *The Duty of Delight,* 16–17

51 Many young people   *Dorothy Day: A Radical Devotion,* 97

52 How to lift the heart   *On Pilgrimage,* 79

53 Now don't think that I've lost my mind   *The Long Loneliness,* 4–5
(From Robert Coles's introduction to the 1997 Harper San Francisco edition)

54 Dryness and lack of recollection   *All the Way to Heaven,* 154

Chapter 10

55 Late this afternoon   *From Union Square to Rome,* 115

56 "But," I reasoned with myself   *The Long Loneliness,* 132–33

It is certainly borne in upon us   *The Catholic Worker,* February 1971

A Way of Life

Chapter 11

61 I'm still in Acts   *The Long Loneliness,* 34

62 The longer I live   *Dorothy Day: A Radical Devotion,* 29

But there is no point   *Dorothy Day: A Radical Devotion,* 126–27

63 The main thing is   *All the Way to Heaven,* 78

The choice is not between   *On Pilgrimage,* 163

64 I have come to the conclusion   *All the Way to Heaven,* 200

We should hunger and thirst   *The Duty of Delight,* 102

65 Our desire for justice   *The Long Loneliness,* 59

For years, in houses of hospitality   *On Pilgrimage,* 189

66 Going to confession   *The Long Loneliness,* 10

It has always seemed to me   *All the Way to Heaven,* 378

67 To be simple as little children   *All the Way to Heaven,* 139–40

I try to think back   *Dorothy Day: A Radical Devotion,* 16

Chapter 12

68 Men and women have persisted   *The Catholic Worker,* May 1978

69 The solution proposed   *The Catholic Worker,* April 1950

And now I pick up   *By Little and by Little,* 181–82

71 What a paradox it is   *The Catholic Worker,* January 1951

73 Much as we want to   *From Union Square to Rome,* 5

We are told to put on Christ   *The Catholic Worker,* July–August 1953

74 One of the greatest evils   *Loaves and Fishes,* 176

Charles de Foucauld died   *All the Way to Heaven,* 330–31

A coworker wrote to me   *All the Way to Heaven,* 142

75 I have been upset with myself   *Dorothy Day: A Radical Devotion,* 120

76 You sounded, too, so discouraged   *All the Way to Heaven,* 112

77 I was thinking   *The Duty of Delight,* 318

What with being sick this week   *The Duty of Delight,* 26

78 Meditation on the bus   *The Duty of Delight,* 31

79 I need some time alone   *The Duty of Delight,* 63

One of the objections to suffering   *The Duty of Delight,* 30

80 I seem angry when I am silent   *The Duty of Delight,* 173–74

Chapter 13

81 I don't only think of the Passion   *Dorothy Day: A Radical Devotion,* 117

82 Christ Our Lord came   *The Catholic Worker,* November 1936

83 When we suffer   *From Union Square to Rome,* 11
The only answer to this mystery   *On Pilgrimage,* 227

84 What unbearable suffering   *By Little and by Little,* 184

85 I have been visiting families   *All the Way to Heaven,* 316

86 How to draw a picture   *On Pilgrimage,* 225
How suffering drives us to prayer!   *The Duty of Delight,* 536

87 If it were not for scripture   *The Duty of Delight,* 524
Compassion – it is a word meaning   *On Pilgrimage,* 224

88 I write to comfort others   *On Pilgrimage,* 228
In patience you will possess   *The Duty of Delight,* 474–75

Chapter 14

89 On the one hand   *On Pilgrimage,* 250–51

90 How I love the park   *The Long Loneliness,* 64
Mass at eight   *The Duty of Delight,* 337
One line of a psalm   *The Catholic Worker,* October–November 1976

91 I owe great thanks to God   *The Duty of Delight,* 515–16

92 This month of thanksgiving   *The Catholic Worker,* November 1936

93 Books to read in wartime   *The Duty of Delight,* 65

94 The song thrilled in my heart   *The Long Loneliness,* 29

95 One thing I kept thinking of   *The Duty of Delight,* 223
This morning at six   *All the Way to Heaven,* 328

96 We want to be happy   *By Little and by Little,* 102

A Way of Community

Chapter 15

99 Do we get much help   *Loaves and Fishes,* 90–91

100 Last week a woman   *On Pilgrimage,* 200–1

101 Failures   *On Pilgrimage,* 202

102 Let us rejoice in poverty   *On Pilgrimage,* 250

Chapter 16

104 The only answer in this life   *Loaves and Fishes*, 243

105 Whenever I groan within myself   *On Pilgrimage*, 123

106 We were in California   *From Union Square to Rome*, 23

107 Children look at things   *The Long Loneliness*, 39

108 Peter Maurin, founder of a movement   *On Pilgrimage*, 83

A philosophy of work   *On Pilgrimage*, 151–52

109 Peter's plan was that groups   *The Long Loneliness*, 225

Community – that was the social answer   *The Long Loneliness*, 224

110 I still think that the only solution   *By Little and by Little*, 280

I think of you all so often   *All the Way to Heaven*, 295

111 We must practice   *The Catholic Worker*, February 1940

Chapter 17

112 Do not be afraid   *All the Way to Heaven*, 108

113 It is important that we try   *All the Way to Heaven*, 146

Saint John the Baptist   *Loaves and Fishes*, 92

115 True love is delicate   *On Pilgrimage*, 239–40

116 A community is not a place   *Dorothy Day: A Radical Devotion*, 130–31

117 Youth demands the heroic   *On Pilgrimage*, 236–37

118 We suffer these things   *Loaves and Fishes*, 84–85

120 We are communities in time   *Dorothy Day: A Radical Devotion*, 109

We cannot love God   *The Long Loneliness*, 285–86

Bibliography

Coles, Robert. *Dorothy Day: A Radical Devotion.* New York: Addison Wesley, 1987.

Day, Dorothy. *All the Way to Heaven: The Selected Letters of Dorothy Day.* Edited by Robert Ellsberg. New York: Image Books, 2010.

_____. *By Little and by Little: The Selected Writings of Dorothy Day.* Edited by Robert Ellsberg. New York: Alfred A. Knopf, 1983.

_____. *The Duty of Delight: The Diaries of Dorothy Day.* Edited by Robert Ellsberg. New York, Image Books, 2011.

_____. *From Union Square to Rome.* Maryknoll, NY: Orbis Books, 2006.

_____. *House of Hospitality.* New York: Sheed & Ward, 1939.

_____. *Loaves and Fishes.* Maryknoll, NY: Orbis Books, 1997.

_____. *The Long Loneliness: The Autobiography of Dorothy Day.* San Francisco: Harper & Row, 1980.

_____. *On Pilgrimage.* Grand Rapids, MI: Wm. B. Eerdmans, 1999.

Forest, Jim. *Love Is the Measure: A Biography of Dorothy Day.* Maryknoll, NY: Orbis Books, 1986.

Acknowledgements

Excerpts from *Loaves and Fishes* by Dorothy Day, copyright © 1963 by Dorothy Day. Reprinted by permission of HarperCollins Publishers.

Excerpts from *The Long Loneliness* by Dorothy Day, illustrated by Fritz Eichenberg, copyright © 1952 by Harper & Row, Publishers, Inc., copyright renewed © 1980 by Tamar Teresa Hennessy. Introduction copyright © 1997 by Robert Coles. Reprinted by permission of HarperCollins Publishers.

Excerpts from *Dorothy Day: Selected Writings,* edited by Robert Ellsberg, copyright © 1983, 1992, 2005 by Robert Ellsberg and Tamar Hennessey. Published in 2005 by Orbis Books, Maryknoll, New York 10545.

Excerpts from *Dorothy Day: A Radical Devotion* by Robert Coles, copyright © 1987 by Robert Coles. Reprinted by permission of Addison Wesley, a member of the Perseus Books Group.

Excerpts from *All the Way to Heaven: The Selected Letters of Dorothy Day,* edited by Robert Ellsberg, copyright © 2010 by Marquette University Press, Milwaukee, Wisconsin, USA. Used by permission of the publisher. All rights reserved. www.marquette.edu/mupress

Excerpts from *The Duty of Delight: The Diaries of Dorothy Day,* edited by Robert Ellsberg, copyright © 2008 Marquette University Press, Milwaukee, Wisconsin, USA. Used by permission of the publisher. All rights reserved.

Scripture quotes at chapter headings are taken from the Holy Bible, New International Version. Copyright © 1973, 1978, 1984, 2011 by Biblica, Inc. Used by permission. All rights reserved worldwide.

All other Bible quotes follow the original sources. Bible references within the text have been added by the editor.

Front cover art copyright © by Julia Lonneman.

Portrait of Dorothy Day (gelatin silver print) on page v by Fritz Kaeser. Reproduced by permission of the Snite Museum of Art of the University of Notre Dame.

Related Titles from Plough

The Prayer God Answers
Eberhard Arnold *and* Richard Foster
Rediscover the kind of prayer that has the power to transform our
lives and our world.

Called to Community
The Life Jesus Wants for His People
Edited by Charles E. Moore
Fifty-two readings on living in intentional Christian community to
spark group discussion.

Discipleship
Living for Christ in the Daily Grind
J. Heinrich Arnold
Sometimes sensitive, sometimes provocative, but always
encouraging, Arnold guides readers toward leading Christlike lives
amid the stress and strain of modern life.

Why We Live in Community
Eberhard Arnold *and* Thomas Merton
In this time-honored manifesto Arnold and Merton join the vital
discussion of what community is all about: a great adventure of faith
shared with others.

Plough Publishing House
1-800-521-8011 ◆ 845-572-3455
PO BOX 398 ◆ Walden, NY 12586 ◆ USA
Brightling Rd ◆ Robertsbridge ◆ East Sussex TN32 5DR ◆ UK
4188 Gwydir Highway ◆ Elsmore, NSW 2360 ◆ Australia

www.plough.com